LEADING
OUT
RETAIL

A Creative Look At Bicycle Retail
And What All Retailers Can Learn From It

Donny Perry

Copyright

Printed in the United States of America, f-yeah.
First Edition: March 2014
I1972ACCUWS2PBAMC4ACTDNC

ISBN: 978-0-9960373-0-3
ISBN: 0996037306

leadingoutretail.com
You can connect with the author on Twitter @donnyperry

For all the bike retailers I've had the pleasure to work with.

Enormous thanks to my friends and coworkers at Specialized.
You're all in here somewhere.

And Amber, ILY.

Table of Contents

Preface

This book could not have been written without the dedicated assistance and support of my colleagues at Specialized Bicycles. My closest colleagues in SBCU (Scott Holz, Corrine Boderman, Julie Bates, Aaron Post, Adam Nicholson, Sean Madsen, George Lee, Tony Baumann, John Friedrich, Hugo Teixeira, Brennan Marquez, Kevin Wilde, Richard "Neon" Salaman, and Sean Xie) offered an invaluable amount of feedback when putting this book together. To them all, I give an enormous amount of gratitude for their help, research, and ideas.

Mike Sinyard and Andy Pruitt were indispensable and offered great mentorship throughout the project. I met them both five years ago and it has been a pleasure having them as sounding boards for so many of my ideas.

Chad Kriz and LeAnne Snyder were wonderful to work with on the design of the book. Chad is one of those rare designers that can take my clustered thoughts and convey them in a simple and beautiful way. LeAnne's photograph of me on the back cover and my Amazon author's page is one of my favorites.

Throughout my career I've had the good fortune of working with so many bike retailers I could write another book just to list and credit each of them. However, I will make a special call out to Marcus Moore at Yojimbos Garage in Chicago, Forrest Ridgway at Bike World, and Greg Rasmussen at Rasmussen Bike Shop- both in West Des Moines. The latter was the last bike shop I worked at before I moved to California to start a career at Specialized. Rasmussen Bike Shop, or Rassy's, will always be my home shop, and I could never thank them enough for their support.

Special thanks to Kale and Shasta at Bicycle Haus, Erik and Dave at Erik's Bike and Board, Matt at Mike's Bikes, Trevin and Nate at The Bike Way, and Dale at Village Bike & Fitness. These retailers are top of their class and it is an absolute pleasure to learn from them.

For a large portion of the data in this book I have pulled from two sources. First, the U.S. Specialty Bicycle Retail Channel 2013 Study and Report and second, the U.S. Bicycle Market 2012 report. Both were prepared by The Gluskin Townley Group on behalf of the National Bicycle Dealers Association. For anyone looking for an understanding of bike retail I strongly encourage you to purchase these reports. Additionally, all sources are credited in the References and Notes section.

There is an old adage that says, 'behind every great man is a great woman'. I prefer to believe that a great woman can turn any man great. I owe so much to Amber Duran for her support, ideas, shoulder, and patience as I wrote this book. She is without doubt, the greatest woman I could have ever hoped for.

Lastly, I owe thanks to you for taking the time to read this. It always amazes me when I write something and even one person takes the time to consume it. That said, this is a self-published piece and if there are any typos or grammatical errors they are entirely my own.

If there are any questions, ideas, or thoughts as you read feel free to contact me on Twitter, @donnyperry .

Prologue

"Listen up! The situation has changed. I'll explain later."
- Captain America. Marvel Super Heroes Secret Wars. Volume 1, #7

Why write a book about bike retail?

Let me start by telling you some of my core beliefs when discussing retail. First, I believe that the world of retail is undergoing the sort of change you only see every 70-100 years. It is the type of change that will force many to think of their store in a whole new context. Second, I believe that retailers who are prepared and open to moving laterally in their business have a chance to survive and even thrive through this paradigm shift. Third, I believe that over the next decade many bike retailers will go out of business and that presents a unique growth opportunity for those that don't. Fourth, I believe that over the next decade new retailers will emerge with business models that seem impossible to understand. Finally, I believe that every process, procedure, and method we have been using for the last 100 years should be scrutinized and reimagined in every way possible.

I am writing this in early 2014 and as proof of this reimagined world of retail, Amazon has recently announced their patent on anticipatory shipping. The idea being that Amazon, and Amazon alone, will have the ability to ship products to their consumers before they order them. The software will pour through the analytics of every consumer's behavior, considering their previous orders, product searches, wish lists, shopping cart contents, returns, and even how long a cursor lingers over an item. Of course these products may be delivered by an Amazon quadcopter drone to the home or office within thirty minutes of the order being placed.

Some of the world's strongest retailers are under extreme stress during this time of change. They are not under stress because they are unintelligent or oblivious to the changing market. They are under stress because of their unwillingness or inability to let go of old business models and move into a new world of retail. During an episode of Weekend Update on Saturday Night Live, Seth Meyers said "Toys-R-Us announced this week that its stores will remain open for 87 straight hours leading up to Christmas. Not to be outdone, the internet announced that it will be open all the time always forever." While it is mockery, it also beautifully illustrates a great retailer bragging about their old-world ways of working.

Bike retailers will not be impervious to this change, they will be affected. In this book I hope to explore strategies and tactics for small-to-medium sized retailers, specifically bike retailers, to prepare them and give them the confidence to make those lateral moves in business. With this book I hope to give retailers a vision of the future, a strategy to approach it, and tactical steps to take right now.

1

I Was Just Riding Along

How can you be sick? You have a mustache.
- David, from the movie American Flyers

If you perform a Google image search for *"I was just riding along"* you will find an endless stream of people crashing on their bikes, snapped frames, folded wheels, cracked handlebars, shredded tires, and bloody skin. The phrase, "I was just riding along" is an anthem for thousands of customers who have brought a destroyed bike to their local retailer absolutely befuddled to how the destruction could have happened. They present the bike to the staff and say, "I was just riding along and (insert level of destruction impossible to achieve by just riding along here)"

The phrase is so ingrained in bike shop culture that there are stores in Maryland, Massachusetts, Florida, and Pennsylvania named Just Riding Along or JRA. There are JRA cycling clubs and many people are selling JRA t-shirts. At Surf City Cyclery in Huntington Beach, California there is an enormous sign hanging above the service area with the phrase for everyone to see.[1] When Surf City's customers say they were just riding along, everyone working can make a polite nod to the sign above. During my own career in bike retail I've seen some amazing JRA moments, here are my top three:

1. A customer brought in a bike and the cranks arms were dragging on the floor, still intact and perfectly mounted through the bottom bracket. He told me he "was just riding along and bottom of the bike fell off". It had turned out the tubes connecting at the bottom bracket had completely rusted through. After asking a few questions I learned the bike had been stored on an outdoor porch through the past decade of winters and summers.

2. A local triathlete brought in his bike and told me, "I was just riding along and noticed there was a hole in my top tube". He forgot to mention that he rode the bike in his heated basement, more than twenty hours a week, and never bothered to clean the sweat that had fallen onto the bike. The sweat had eaten its way through the frame.

3. A father brought his son into the shop demanding a refund. Apparently his son was "just riding along" when the front half of the bike was separated from the back half. I was confused at how it could happen and felt even worse when I told him that the issue was not covered by warranty. He left the store furious, cursing, and threatening to sue. He returned the next day and apologized as he had learned that his son jumped the bike from the roof of their garage. We both had a good laugh.

When it comes to a JRA moment, customers often don't know or can't see what they're doing incorrectly. Perhaps they weren't taught what to look for or maybe they're just oblivious to the fatigue and use their bike is going through. But a true JRA moment is something any experienced technician worth their salary can spot months and possibly years before it will happen. Technicians will notice when riders have been shifting under load while climbing or when a chain hasn't been cleaned and lubed after riding in the rain. Technicians will easily see when someone is riding on tires that are not inflated properly or worse, on suspension that hasn't been properly set up. And yes, they will notice- like I did -when a bike has been hucked off a roof. To the customer's credit a bike can be confusing, but with some small changes in behavior and an understanding of basic maintenance the bike will last them for decades.

Bike shop owners, managers, technicians or anyone else who has done some time in bike retail will understand how to prevent a JRA moment on a bike, but will they know how to prevent a JRA moment in their business? Would they be able to notice if the business is driving toward failure? What are the signals to look for? What are the cues? Do retailers know the small changes in behavior they can make to ensure their business is healthy and working properly for many years to come?

In a 2013 survey of 279 independent bicycle retailers, 58% of them claimed to not have an annual budget for their business, a statistic that would make any first year business student drop their jaw.[2] These retailers may be the most susceptible to a JRA business failure. It is not surprising that this lack of planning happens either, I meet many owners and managers who tell me they are cyclists first and retailers second. While there is nothing wrong with this, I remind them that they can't afford for retailing to be a distant second. As the race unfolds, it's got to stay close. This book is a series of philosophies and business ideas that will get cyclists thinking as retailers first and help them avoid any oncoming JRA moments.

Sadly the JRA moment has already struck hundreds of bike retailers in the US. In any major city the data suggests that very soon one-third of all bike retailers will go out of business. According to the National Bicycle Dealer Association (NBDA) the number of retailers in the United States since 2000 has decreased by 2140. Here is the annual breakdown.[3]

2014

2000: 6195
2001: 6259
2002: 5505
2003: 5358
2004: 4982
2005: 4704
2006: 4599
2007: 4451
2008: 4394
2009: 4319
2010: 4256
2011: 4178
2012: 4089
2013: 4055

It is important to note that this decline in bike retailers has happened despite significant changes to the contrary. In every state since 2000 bicycling infrastructure has improved. From 1992 to 1999 the US Department of Transportation dedicated only $2.9 million toward recreational trail programs. Why this may seem like a lot, in comparison they dedicated $191.8 million between 2000 and 2012.[4] Meaning it is now much easier for people to use their bikes. There are also more bike lanes, bike trails, and cycling advocacy groups in the country. Public transit in nearly every major city has embraced cycling and allows people to take a bike on a bus or train.[5] Gasoline prices have increased and the costs of maintaining an automobile have skyrocketed.[6] The three largest bicycle manufacturers, Specialized, Trek, and Giant have all grown considerably in the past decade.[7]

The sporting side of cycling has grown as well, in 2000 there were 122,388 people that entered a triathlon and by 2012 the number had risen to 550,446.[8] USA Cycling sold nearly 32,000 more memberships in 2012 than it did in 2002. In that same time period the number of sanctioned cycling clubs in the country nearly doubled; growing from 1438 to 2812.[9]

By every other measure cycling is a healthy and growing sport in the US. How is it possible that the sport of cycling has grown so much but the number of bike shops has dropped by over 35%?

In my work I have learned that retailers (all types of retailers, not just bike retailers) have an incredible amount of hindsight and insight when it comes to their business, but not much foresight. Looking at the steady decline of bike retailers in the US, one would be led to ask, "What type of change would need to occur in the industry, country, or culture to turn this decline around?" If there is something that will reverse this pattern; I am not smart enough to see it. If we assume that this pattern of decline will continue for next 15 years we will see another 35% loss of bike retailers. A mathematician might map it out like this:

2014: 3889
2015: 3796
2016: 3702
2017: 3609
2018: 3515
2019: 3422
2020: 3328
2021: 3235
2022: 3142
2023: 3048
2024: 2955

2025: 2861

2026: 2768

2027: 2675

2028: 2597

However I believe the change will be faster. The drop in the number of bike retailers is not going to be linear, it will be exponential. This is because independent, brick and mortar bike retailers are going to get hit from three sides. First, a larger amount of customers will choose online channels for research, and ultimately purchasing. The amount of accessible information combined with the ease of purchase has surpassed the capabilities of nearly every brick and mortar retailer. Evans Cycles in the U.K. sells bikes both online and through one of their 50+ locations. In a recent survey they asked riders where they purchased their last bike and 26.6% purchased online.[10] If we compare Evans Cycles to Target, where online sales account for less than 2% of their total revenue,[11] it would appear that when given the option many cyclists are very comfortable not visiting a store to purchase their bike.

Some retailers suggest that with the growth of online purchasing the era of loyalty is gone. That customers used to be loyal to their local bike shop, and now they are just shopping based on price. I would disagree and instead suggest that customers were never as loyal as originally thought, they were just limited by selection. The local bike shop was their only source for information and the only place they could buy the product. Now with limitless selection, they're spreading their dollar around and being more selective with whom they purchase from.

The second place retailers are going to get hit is by manufacturers that prefer to sell directly to the rider. Currently, every product needed to become a cyclist is offered, in some form, direct from a manufacturer or through an online retailer.

Apparel companies have proven that bike retailers are not needed to be successful at selling high-dollar, premier cycling apparel. Nearly every company making helmets will sell that helmet directly from their website and dozens of bike brands can be purchased through online retailers like Competitive Cyclist, Chain Reaction, or Wiggle. Like all other retail goods, shopping for cycling gear has never been easier.

The third challenge is bikes will become simpler to assemble, use, and maintain. Twenty years ago buying wheels meant having to carefully select hubs, spokes, and rims and then waiting weeks for a master wheel builder to assemble them. Today, having a set of wheels built from the ground up is reserved for only those truly dedicated to customization. Wheels are prebuilt and when they're damaged it can often mean replacement, not repair. Even the most common repairs will be disrupted and as cycling technology advances riders won't need bike shops for derailleur or brake adjustments either. We are in early days of electronic components and it will not be long before the simplest of adjustments are done by using an app, not a wrench.

How people will use a bike shop will make a drastic change in the next decade. When we respond to consumer demands, bike retail will move from a place that supplies goods to a place that offers unique services and cultivates a connection to the cycling community. Many retailers will struggle with this change and choose to close up shop. Others will be forced out if they cannot adapt quickly enough, but those who survive the next decade will live through the most dynamic and lasting change the world of retail will ever see.

I have had the fortunate privilege to work with thousands of bike retailers and have visited over 500 bike retailers in 20 countries. I have seen neighborhood bike shops operating out of garages and organizations that have locations scattered across several states. Working with that many retailers I began to see the commonalities; the things they all do great, and the places where they all struggle. I have also noticed when a retailer does something that sets them apart from everyone else; the one thing a they do better than any other retailer in the world. For some bike shops their "one thing" will be employee management or community engagement. For others it will be much simpler, perhaps they are the ones who have developed the best way to store cables and housing or they may be the best on social media. Interestingly though, very few retailers will know what their crown skill is. They simply never have the opportunity to spend time in other bike shops and use them as a comparison. Without that comparison, many retailers never knew what they were better or worse at.

This was my motivation for writing this book. If I wrote down what I have seen as the best practices for bike retailers from around the world, then we could all learn from each other and be more equipped to survive the next decade of change. In a world of independent retailers, now more than ever we need a common level of service and experience. We would benefit immensely from industry wide standards on how to perform service, sales, and community building. I believe that if we continue without it, online shopping and sporting industry giants will continue to have the upper hand. They will be able to move faster, they will be better funded, and they will have better insights which will allow them to deliver a consistent experience to their customers. Without a level of consistency and cooperation among independent bicycle retailers, I believe the entire industry is at risk of being disrupted. This disruption can be a very healthy thing, but only for those who are prepared.

We are living through one of the most dramatic and changing times in retail history. 20 years from now, in retrospect, no one will disagree. We are seeing tremendous change in how people buy and what people expect from a retail experience. This book was written as a roadmap for the local bike shop during this time of disruption. Plenty of people are offering strategic advice, they are shouting to grow community or engage customers in a different way, and I am sure their advice is spot on. However, what they are not teaching is how to do it. With this book I have no intention of offering only strategic advice; my aim is to provide simple, tactical processes for improving business and preparing for the next era of retail. I will show how to implement procedures that will result in faster transactions, higher average sales, and most importantly how to create greater engagement with customers. To do this I will use firsthand experience from over 15 years in the industry combined with anecdotal stories from all types of industries. I will also deliver this information in an easy-to-read and simple to use format.

Thomas Edison said, "Genius is one percent inspiration, ninety-nine percent perspiration."[12] Implying that anyone can have an idea but very few can bring that idea to life. Ideas, in the relative scheme of things, are easy. Taking an idea to fruition on the other hand is very difficult. The number one challenge anyone faces with retail is implementation of great ideas. Many bike retailers are very fortunate. Vendors go out of their way to create national marketing campaigns, merchandising tools, sales tools, sales training, and other resources. These are the kind of assets that a lot of independent retailers simply do not get.

Despite all of these tools it can still be very difficult to implement them. Most of the tools vendors supply will sit firmly in the category of the one-percent, they are just great ideas. Implementing those tools and using them to increase sales or customer satisfaction sits in the ninety-nine percent category. It is hard and laborious work.

I will make no illusions here, this book is a one percent piece. It is packed with ideas but it cannot implement anything. Without a ninety-nine percent effort, this book is just an interesting use of time and money. My hope is that retailers will read the book, pick the ideas that are best for their business, and then go after them with complete aggression to see them through. To quote Edison again, "Everything comes to him who hustles while he waits."[13]

Kansas City Shuffle

"The local bike shop will survive. The customer service game has to be upheld and get higher in order to compete against online sales. Dealers will have to be attentive to pricing but still remain profitable...You cannot bring your bike into an online store, but you can bring it into your local bike shop. And, I bet the trip to your local shop will be a bit more fun than a trip on the world wide web."

Jon Franzky of Bow Cycles said this in a January 2013 interview with pinkbike.com.[14] Since Franzky has placed his focus on service, it is not likely that he has been misguided like so many other bike retailers. Many of whom are victims to the Kansas City Shuffle.

A Kansas City Shuffle refers to a con game using misdirection and subterfuge- when everyone looks left, you go right. It could be argued that over the past decade brick and mortar retailers were caught up in the history's largest Kansas City Shuffle. When online retailers started to make their presence known by giving customers another option to buy their goods, the leading argument from all brick and mortar retailers at the time was price. They argued that online retailers were pricing products too low or too high or that they didn't pay taxes. They would debate that while the product may have been cheap the shipping costs would make it more expensive. They proclaimed that customers want to buy it and take it home today. While brick and mortar retailers were focused on pricing and delivery they may have missed what online retailers were really doing, creating a new and arguably better customer service experience.

In the same interview on pinkbike.com Matt Cole from the online retailer Chain Reaction Cycles said this, "We have a 12-month, 365-day hassle-free returns service, a full warranty policy, a 120-man strong customer service team who can be contacted via email or phone made up of a highly qualified Tech Team with all the bike knowledge anyone could ask for and an international group of advisors on hand who can offer support in seven different languages, including Japanese, Russian, French, Italian, Spanish, Portuguese and German."

Cole isn't talking about price instead he's talking about customer service. This type of customer service can cover a wide breadth of products with a serious depth of knowledge at the same time. Add to that, it is a type of service that can be customized to every rider who walks through their virtual doors. Cole goes on to say,

"Our goal is to have the most enriched content online so that customers are equipped with all the details they need to make a purchase. We aim to have product specs and descriptions, 360-degree image views, video buyer's guides, fit guides, and size guides where applicable and we have a dedicated Tech Team who are on hand to offer technical support whether you've got a straightforward question on crank compatibility or an in-depth query on bleeding your disc brakes. We always welcome feedback so we can continue to furnish our customers with all the information they need."

While Franzky is focused on the service his brick and mortar can provide, Cole wants to speak to his customers long before they walk into Franzky's store. The more Cole can convince his visitors that he is an authority on the products he is selling the greater his odds of making the sale. And once the sale is made and the snowball has been pushed down the hill, it will only grow.

Franzky was correct in saying "you can't bring your bike into an online store". Service is what will keep bike shops strong over the next decade of change but I would argue that it can't be the usual service we've been doing. Customers deserve better, they expect better, and retailers should start exploring every type of service that results in a unique and customized experience.

To prove that the Kansas City Shuffle has worked, simply look to the investments that bike retailers have made into the services they offer. If service is how bike shops will win people over, why haven't the services the bike industry offers changed much in the past 20 years? In an article posted on Bicycle Retailer and Industry News author Fred Clements wrote "High-profit stores report 11.4 percent of their revenue comes from repair parts and labor, compared to only 6.5 percent for the average. The emphasis on the service department may be even more significant going forward. As Internet sellers continue to challenge brick-and-mortar for product sales, some of the difference may be made up in areas where Internet sellers find it difficult or impossible to compete."[15] Clements prediction is correct, if companies like Chain Reaction have their way and dominate the sale of products, bike shops will be forced to live on the smallest percentage of their business; service.

It is not difficult to imagine a world where all the products sold at a bike retailer were also sold online (for many this is not imaginary, it's reality). In that world the only thing left for retailers to sell at a decent profit margin is service. In order to operate a bike shop on such a small slice of total revenue as service, retailers would need to start planning three things. First, build a strategy for how to take service dollars from competing bike shops in their market. Increasing the average sale that the service department is currently doing may not be enough (though it is important), many will want new customers as well. If the pie isn't going to get bigger, how can one bike shop cut themselves a larger slice? If a bike retailer is currently earning $100,000 from the service department, they will need six or seven bike shops in the market, doing the same volume, to completely shut down. It's a tall order but it is where we are headed.

Second, retailers will need to build a plan for how to differentiate service so no one else can offer anything similar. If the shopping and service experience is practically identical between two bike retailers, one of them will need to strive to be better and different. The goal is to give the customer something they can point to and say, "I go to this bike shop because they are the only ones who do _____".

Third, start selling new types of services. Many bike shops have jumpstarted this trend in the past decade by offering more bike fitting. A bike fit can include, but is not limited to, pedal stroke analysis, building a custom shoe, and even building a custom bike. When the labor dollars from bike fitting can be as much as 5% of total revenue, it is service worth investing in.

Here are some examples of how bike shops have placed a focus on providing a unique service.

Wheatridge Cyclery. Denver, Colorado. Walking into Wheatridge Cyclery one may notice that near the front door there are three stations that, at first glance, appear to be set up for bike fitting. Actually, these stations are solely for bike sizing (quickly adjusting the saddle height and handlebar position prior to a test ride). Nearly half of the second floor is dedicated to five, fully equipped, fitting stations. The crew at Wheatridge Cyclery understand that a bike fitter working for two hours has the potential to earn twice as much as a bike mechanic working for two hours, so they have taken the idea to the next logical step. By answering the question, how much can be earned if there were several bike fitters working at the same time?

Faster. Scottsdale, Arizona. Faster claims that they are cycling's most comprehensive performance center. Founder James

Kramer says on their website, "What we see here, which was launched in August of 2011 is the culmination of 18 months' worth of vision-casting and planning. [Faster is] boutique retail for road cyclists and triathletes, high end maintenance and service, world class bike fit, performance testing and nutritional evaluation, a full suite of recovery services, and then anchored by what we call the 'secret sauce' the world's first low speed wind tunnel developed specifically for cycling."[16] At Faster, it is quickly apparent that they are not in the business of selling products that require services, instead they sell services that are made better when customers purchase their products. This is a massive shift from how most bike retailers think and operate, but a necessary shift in order to truly differentiate.

One On One. Minneapolis, Minnesota. At One On One customers going to notice something different. Tables and chairs, local art displayed as if it were a museum, a fully functional coffee bar and kitchen, plus a wall covered with the stuffed heads of ten point bucks (framesets delicately displayed in their antlers). It's not the normal bike shop. One On One sells and fixes bikes like any other bike shop but they do it while offering a completely different experience. It is easy to get lost in the local art while drinking an organic, fair trade coffee. Meet people for lunch and grab a sandwich or soup. When it comes to bikes One On One has rental bikes and an always changing selection of used bikes to offer. When someone needs something more specific they are invited to spend an entire day searching through "the junkyard". A basement filled with bins of old cycling parts (tools are not allowed in the junkyard). If a bike needs to be repaired One on One does not offer a standard $55 tune-up, instead they have a $1 per minute rate. However many minutes it takes, that's how much it costs.

Ride Studio Café. Lexington, Massachusetts. Just outside of Boston Ride Studio Café (RSC) is a unique combination of bike shop and café. Though their coffee is great that isn't the only thing that makes them special. On their website they state that their "mission is to create a service experience that has never existed in the bike industry."[17] They do this by offering extended hours; 7am-7pm on weekdays and 8am-6pm on the weekends. 24-hour or same day services on repairs and pick up or delivery to the home or office. They go above and beyond by offering a personal shopper service where they will schedule an appointment to walk their customers through the products they sell and help them find products that perfectly suit their tastes. Once they've determined which products someone likes they can be added to a customized email group and get notified when new products arrive that they might enjoy.

These stores are just the tip of the iceberg in bike retailers that are making the shift from selling bikes to creating amazing service experiences. They understand that service is not just how to treat someone, what types of questions to ask, or how to fix a flat tire. With all the different ways to structure one's business I would encourage retailers to not shy away from the fringes. A retailer can spend the next decade trying to increase margin on products by .015% or they can run year-long a benchmarking study to learn how to perform a derailleur adjustment better than the guy down the street- but this type of work is piddling and would be a waste of time. Instead, I challenge retailers to completely change the game by offering something unique and unexpected. In essence, run a Kansas City Shuffle.

We Need A Great Leadout
Not A Salesperson

In November of 2012 Gallup conducted a poll where participants were asked to rate the honesty and ethical standards of people in different fields of work. While the highest rated professions are nurses, doctors, and engineers- the lowest scores were given to salesmen.[18] Even members of Congress are perceived as more trustworthy than a salesman. This is why I have such disdain for the title. Once someone is called a salesperson, even they may not be able to overcome the perception of what a salesperson is. Some of the most common adjectives used when describing a salesperson are pushy, aggressive, slimy, sleazy, dishonest, manipulative, and fake. This perception can be very difficult to overcome. It is an easy trap to believe that a salesperson's work is somehow dishonest and conniving. For this reason I have always disliked using the words sales, salesperson, and sales floor. While it clearly explains the job it also carries too many negative connotations.

If a photo is worth a thousand words then I believe that an effective brand can be worth a thousand photos. Which led me to the question; can we drastically change the behavior of our staff if we rebrand them? Instead of calling our staff salespeople, I prefer to give them the title, "Leadout".

In professional road cycling a leadout is when one cyclist drives the pace at the front, working for their team leader by blocking the wind and allowing them to conserve energy in their draft. Just before the finish line the person giving the leadout moves out of the way giving the team leader a clear shot to victory. In the bike shop I see the primary role of the people working is to be a leadout for their customers. To give their energy and guidance in helping every customer achieve their goal.

Once people start to think of themselves as leadouts, they begin to think much more clearly about their role and duties. The job isn't to sell a bike, the job as a leadout is to make sure the customer has the best bike for what they need to achieve. The job isn't to ring them out at the cash register and wish them a great day. A leadout knows that the work is not done until the customers have crossed their personal finish line and raised their arms in victory. A salesman sells, a leadout leads.

To solidify this idea, throughout the book I will refer to a salesperson, salesman, or saleswoman as a leadout but I won't stop there. I will use terminology that will redefine each role within the bike business. Instead of saying sales floor, I will say "retail area". Instead of selling, I will be "leading". Instead of calling people mechanics, I will call them "technicians" Instead of workshops, I will say "service area". I'm looking to rebrand bike retail in our minds and our customers' minds as well. Which leads to the one title I hate the most- dealer.

In the bicycle industry many retailers refer to themselves as an IBD or Independent Bicycle Dealer. IBDs have often classified their work as selling bicycles, bike repair, cycling apparel, tools, and accessories. However the IBD is an aging dinosaur in need of a new moniker.

I believe that there is a difference between an Independent Bicycle Dealer and an Independent Bicycle Retailer (IBR or simply bike retailer). An IBD is a dealer and, just like a drug dealer standing on the corner, they schlep a product. Moving product as fast as possible with little or no concern to who buys it or what they do with it. An IBD doesn't care about the community, an IBD doesn't care about their reputation, and an IBD will do anything to make a sale. The IBD discounts, cuts deals, screws over their vendors and their customers. They look for the easiest way out of everything while trying to snatch every dollar from the people silly enough to buy from them.

An IBR on the other hand is constantly focused on creating a positive shopping experience. They care about the look of their store. They never stop striving to improve the services they offer. They work to cultivate a positive community, and the IBR creates a lasting engagement with their customers. The IBR never needs to cut corners or slice prices, their customers recognize their work and see value in everything they do. The IBR may not be cheaper, but they are different, they are better, and customers see themselves as partners.

Are you an IBD or an IBR?

Timmy

When I work with a group of IBRs one of the first questions I will ask is, "What do you want from your business?" Some will give the classic answer of money, others will say growth, and a few might be more abstract by telling me they're looking for happiness or legacy. Some answers are altruistic; they will say that the community is the reason, or that the sport gave so much to them they had to find a way to give back. For a select few their answer is the opportunity to open up more retail businesses. Surprisingly though, all of these answers would make up only 10% of the responses. By far, the most popular answer I get is when asking what a retailer wants from their business, they say, "I'd like more time to ride my bike."

More time to ride their bike. This answer outweighs spending time with family, time to travel, and time to explore a new passion or idea. Let me speak specifically about the retailers that tell me they'd like to ride their bike more, why I think this is such a popular response, and what it means for bike retail as a whole.

Like many sports industries, the bicycle industry is deeply rooted in the passion of the sport. The overwhelming majority of people who work in bike shops love bikes. They ride bikes, they talk bikes, they breathe bikes, and it is not uncommon to hear them say they bleed bikes. Bikes consume them in every way.

Very few IBRs opened a store because they were passionate about the business of retail, which was never the goal. In their first year of business most IBRs never even considered the challenges of maintaining margin, measuring supply and demand, or launching a marketing campaign. When they were kids they started working in bike shops because they loved it. As adults they couldn't see themselves doing anything else except sharing their love for riding with as many people as possible, and what better way to do that than to sell bikes, fix bikes, and teach people about the freedom and joy of riding.

So when retailers tell me they want more time to ride I hit them with a follow-up question, "Why don't you?" and the answers never stop surprising me. They will tell me that customers prefer to work with them. They tell me that they are the only ones who understand how to perform the daily tasks. They tell me that if they're not there, mistakes are made, quality drops into the toilet, and customer service is compromised. They believe and have years of anecdotal evidence to prove that the business cannot run without them.

I see it a different way. What I see is retailers who do not trust their staff. They are discomforted by the thought of leaving and any ride they go on will just be filled with stress and worry about the store.

As proof of their distrust, when I have worked with employees of a store and asked what their biggest hurdles are, almost unanimously they say that the owner is too scared to let them do anything. It's a classic catch-22, the owner wants to step away but can't until the employees have more experience and prove themselves, but the employees can't gain that experience until the owner steps out of the way.

In 2011 I was working with a group of retailers and we were discussing the types of employees they have working for them. We focused on the employee who was new or seasonal help, the employee who didn't understand a lot of the basics, and the employee that needed more supervision. Every IBR has this employee, so to make the conversation simple I decided to give them a name, their name would be Timmy.

Throughout this book I will refer to Timmy. This is not intended as an insult to anyone who has the same name. It is not a reference to Timmy from the show South Park and I've never known someone named Timmy. My father's name wasn't Timmy and I was never bullied in school by a guy named Timmy. It was just the first name that came to mind, people seemed to remember it, and everyone referred to it easily. By the end of the three day course retailers were telling me that they have two Timmys they plan to have conversations with, another person told me how his Timmy would be attending a class I was teaching, and one even told me how he was planning to terminate Timmy when he got back to the store. The name Timmy stuck in peoples' head, so I ran with it.

It should be stated that Timmy is not dumb or challenged in any way, he is capable of doing anything. He just needs more guidance and a stronger focus from management. Timmy can be male or female. No one is ashamed to have Timmy working at their side, because we were all Timmy at one time. Timmy is simply the lowest common denominator in a bike retail business. Depending on the rest of the staff, Timmy may have a degree in engineering, he may have raced as a pro, or have even been working in the industry for the past decade.

As the lowest common denominator we build our training plans, our processes, and our procedures around Timmy's abilities and capabilities. We build our developmental plans with the hope to bring Timmy up to the level of manager or even owner. We predict our customer service satisfaction based on how Timmy is likely to interact with them. We structure our finances around Timmy's salary and needs. Everything we build in our business, we build with the idea that someday, Timmy may be at the helm.

Since managing people in bike shops today is becoming less about command and control and more about development and empowerment. Increasingly, IBR owners and managers need to give Timmy the knowledge and skills necessary to perform at a high level. To do this, managers are doing less management and more coaching and guidance. As the work in a store is constantly changing, as the demands for a more thorough and specific skillset grow, Timmy needs the skills to adapt to new situations and that adaptation will not come from traditional management, but rather through coaching to build employees' knowledge, skills, deductive reasoning, and communication skills. Unless an owner is handed an entire staff that are all fully capable of performing their job at the highest level, a certain amount of coaching will be needed.

One of the characteristics of great managers is that they groom others. Timmy will require a long-term effort that promotes his development, focuses on interpersonal skills, and creates a positive leadership style. Timmy may also require a fair amount of technical training but this is secondary. We need Timmy to be able to speak to someone who is buying their first bike and not intimidate them. At the same time we need Timmy to speak to an experienced cyclist with a knowledge and insight that garners respect. We need Timmy to perform simple tasks like cleaning and fixing a flat tire. We also need him to perform complex tasks like a hydraulic brake bleed or updating firmware on a shifting system. We need Timmy to be all things to all people.

Building a business with all this in mind is building with complete awareness of the Timmy factor. If we constantly consider the Timmy factor and are capable of building a business where Timmy can be successful- then maybe, just maybe, we could head out for a few more bike rides.

Start With Why

As of December, 2013 Simon Sinek's Ted Talk, How Great Leaders Inspire Action, was ranked number three of most watched Ted Talks with over fourteen million views.[19] And deservingly so, many businesses have used Sinek's talk to guide their strategies. The talk is referenced in dozens of books and Specialized, Trek, and Cannondale have all used the talk in presentations to their retailers. One of the reasons the video is so popular is because Sinek explains how inspired leaders and organizations think differently than everyone else. They do this by first defining why they do what they do. Then they say how they do it and finally, what they do. I will break that down a bit further.

What. Every bike retailer in the world knows what they do. These are the clearest definitions of their business and for many reading this book, the most common list of what bike retailers do:

- Sell bicycles, equipment, and apparel
- Repair bicycles
- Fit bicycles
- Coaching and/or consulting

How. Many bike retailers can even define how they do it. This is what many people in business refer to as their unique selling proposition, or USP. This is what makes doing business with one IBR better than shopping from their competition. Here are the most common answers I hear to how people do what they do.

- Perfect location
- Great selection
- Experienced and highly trained staff
- Family owned
- Detail oriented
- Fastest turn around
- Competitive prices
- Awesome shopping experience
- No intimidation or pushy salespeople

Looking at this list, many retailers will agree that those are all things their business offers to their customers. That's the catch, every IBR believes they offer these things and no owner or manager will say otherwise. No bike retailer in the country will tell their customers, "We have a crappy selection of bikes, moron employees, and we do really shitty work." If everyone is offering the same thing, what makes anyone truly special, different, or unique?

Why. Where companies struggle is defining why they do what they do, and to quote Sinek "It is not to make a profit, that is a result and it is always a result. By *why* I mean, what is your purpose, your cause, or your belief? Why does your organization exist? Why do you get out of bed every morning? And why should anyone care?" When retailers effectively define why they do what they do, they are speaking to the emotional center of their customers. Here are some of the best I have heard.

- We live and breathe triathlon.
- We believe you deserve the best cycling experience.
- We believe the bike should never be an excuse.
- We believe cycling will change your life.
- We want to grow the Portland commuting scene.
- We provide a service with a performance benefit.

- We want more cyclists riding more often.
- We are mountain bikers to the bone.

When retailers define why they do what you do, many of the day-to-day business choices become a lot easier. For example, let's pretend a retailer has defined their why as, "We live and breathe triathlon." What brands do they carry? They carry brands that have a dedicated focus to triathlon. What type of people do they hire? Triathletes, preferably people who live and breathe triathlon. What publications do they advertise in? They advertise in publications that triathletes read. What events do they sponsor? That's easy, they sponsor triathlons. What would be the best way to grow their business? Possibly with swim and run gear. People do not buy from businesses that have what they need; people buy from businesses that believe what they believe.

Be Different

Steve Jobs, the former CEO of Apple, played his cards right by never trying to be cheaper or more accessible than his competitors. He also refused to settle for just having a better product. Offering more memory or computing power was a meaningless race. Instead Jobs pushed Apple to be different. He understood that a successful business can beat their competition by being different, better, or cheaper. They all work, it's just a matter of determining which camp to join. Jobs chose to be different and even echoed this goal in the company's tagline, "Think Different."

Doing things cheaper is the easiest way to grab a sale. Customers all around the world are trained to go for the discounts. Thirty years ago a 5% or 10% discount may have been something to brag about, today discounts from most mass retailers rarely get noticed unless they are 50% off or more. Everyone is looking for the best deal, the biggest price cut, and the two-for-one type of sale. Retailers that aim to be cheaper do so by having an extremely efficient business. They leverage all terms from their vendors, they buy in bulk, and they are constantly trying to cut fixed costs, marketing expenses, and operational expenses. They look for the cheapest staff possible and if the customer could ever serve themselves, it's a wonderful thing.

Being better means understanding competition thoroughly and combating their weaknesses with strengths. Retailers who aim to be better know exactly how they perform a tune-up and add extra steps in their service. If their competition gets it done in five days, they get it done in three. If the competition has two color choices, these retailers have four. If competition does bike sizing, they perform bike fitting. Everything the competition can do, these IBRs believe they can do better.

However, those few who are looking to be different have the greatest edge. Being different means offering a service or product that no one else can offer. Creating an experience that cannot be replicated. Retailers who wish to be different are focused on what differentiates their business, but not just from other IBRs, from all businesses. People are drawn to these retailers and never stop talking about them. Some people love them, some don't, and that is fine with IBRs who are focused on being different. They know they can't be everything to everyone, but those customers who understand them will remain loyal to everything they do.

Retail Industry or
Real Estate Industry?

If we were to center a microscope over brick and mortar retail what many people tend to find is that it's a real estate game just as much as a retail game. If an IBR can earn significant dollars per square feet then they'll have opportunities to set up business in a location with great traffic, parking, and amenities that facilitate a positive shopping experience. If they cannot earn the dollars per square foot then they're blocked out of the prime locations and will work harder to convince customers to seek them out. This is how the phrase, "We're a destination location" was born.

Sales per square foot is a popular metric used in the retailing industry and is simply the average revenue a bike shop creates for every square foot of sales space. Investopedia, a website dedicated to educating people on finances, investing, and more defines sales per square foot like this, "Sales per square foot is used by businesses and analysts alike to measure the efficiency of a store's management in creating revenues with the amount of sales space available to them. The higher the sales per square foot, the better job management is doing of marketing and displaying the store's products."[20]

According to the National Bicycle Dealers Association the average square footage of a bike shop in the United States is 4472 square feet.[21] In a survey done by RetailSails, a retail and consumer goods consulting firm, they measured the average square footage of the nine most successful retailers in the US. They found that the average retail space of Apple, Tiffany, and Coach was similar to bike shops at just under 5000 square feet, the difference was how much those stores earned per square foot- and it was a drastic difference.

Apple was the runaway leader by far, earning $6050 per square foot nearly double over second place Tiffany & Co. The yoga-inspired apparel store Lululemon came in third at $1936 per square foot.[22] And what about bike shops? Depending on their size a bike shop will earn between $100 and $250 per square feet.[23] While most bicycles are more expensive than most Apple products, and require a highly knowledgeable and educated staff, they have the same earning power as a low-end department or a RadioShack.

It's this kind of earning disparity that tells us bike retailers are clearly playing the retail game, not the real estate game. This means there will rarely be a bike retailer next to an Apple store, Tiffany & Co. or even a Lululemon. Most IBRs simply can't afford to run a profitable business in those locations.

Since IBRs are playing the retail game they have to convince people to find them and when they do, the people working at a bike retailer have to win them over with an engaging experience, incredible product knowledgeable, and a rooted sense of trust with all cyclists walking in.

Chapter 1
Vansevenant Checklist

At the end of each chapter I will put together a checklist that summarizes the contents of the chapter. Consider the reading as training and this checklist as a tool for implementing. I have named these checklists after one of my favorite professional cyclists, Wim Vansevenant. He was the only person to finish in last place of the Tour de France three years in a row: 2006, 2007, and 2008.[24] The person who finishes last is known as the lanterne rouge which is French for red lantern. A red lantern used to be hung from the caboose of a train.

Losing as Wim did, so spectacularly, is much harder for a professional rider to accomplish than it sounds. Just as Wim Vansevenant was at the end of the Tour de France, these checklists will be at the end of every chapter. Enjoy.

Are you just riding along in business?

Do you build an annual budget for your store?

Do you have salespeople or do you have Leadouts? Mechanics or technicians? Are you a dealer or a retailer? An IBD or an IBR?

Who is Timmy in your business?

Watch Simon Sinek's TED Talk: http://bit.ly/IoXgYz

Why does your business exist? And why should people care?

Compare to your competition; are you cheaper, better, or different? Explain how.

Are you in the retail industry or the real estate industry?

What are your current sales per square foot?

2

Time for Phase 2:
Pricing & Pareto

"Well just like the rest of us, you have to make choices with your money. Do you want a bike, or do you want to be depressed?"
- Randy Marsh, character from South Park

In the winter of 2000 I took a job as a bike messenger for Kozmo.com. Kozmo was a website where someone could order DVDs and all their basic groceries and have them delivered to their door via messenger within 30 minutes. It was the perfect solution for anyone who was too busy, lazy, drunk, or high to venture out into the world. Need an 11:00pm ice cream fix but don't want to get dressed? No problem, type up Kozmo and they will be right over.

Kozmo was a great idea, and so many people believed in the idea the company saw massive growth in its first three years earning hundreds of millions in seed money. However, while people believed in Kozmo very few actually bought anything from them and their first three years of business were also their last. Since, Kozmo has become an iconic example of businesses that burst with the dot com bubble.[1]

I worked at Kozmo for two weeks and during that time I made four deliveries, two of which were to the same home. It was one of many jobs I have quit out of sheer boredom. During one of my evenings at work I was standing around, as usual, chatting with my supervisor. We were looking out into a warehouse filled with DVDs, huge shelves of food, and refrigerators full of milk, eggs, and ice cream. None of which was going anywhere except to feed the employees while they waited for work to come in. The signs were clear even then, Kozmo could not last. When I asked my supervisor how long he expected the company to survive he told me, "Not long. They haven't figured out Phase 2 yet." When I asked him to explain further he walked over to the shelf full of DVDs, grabbed a season of South Park, handed it to me and said, "Why don't you head home and watch this. I think we can handle the work here."

Two years prior to my time at Kozmo, Matt Stone and Trey Parker were deep into their second season of their classically crude comedy South Park. Episode 17 of the series had a lesson for many of the budding dot com businesses like Kozmo who seemed to be growing out of nothing.[2] It was an important lesson that has a lot of applications and is worth repeating.

In the episode the mayor of South Park asks the boys Eric, Stan, Kyle, and Kenny to give a presentation to the town committee teaching the dangers of supporting Harbucks, a national chain of coffee houses that is moving into South Park. In preparation for their speech the boys stay up late and meet an underpants gnome who makes nightly visits only to steal their underpants. The boys follow the gnome back to his secret lair where they discover an enormous pile of stolen underpants. When the boys ask the gnomes why they're collecting all the underpants, the gnomes present their three phase business plan.

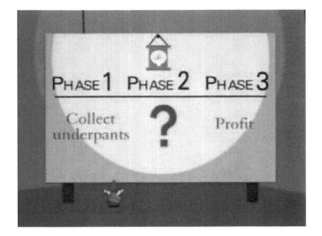

Fig 2.1: The Underpants Gnomes 3-phase business plan.

Phase 1: Collect Underpants
Phase 2: ?
Phase 3: Profit

When the boys press the gnomes to explain phase 2, they realize they have no idea how to turn collected underpants into profit. That is what my Kozmo supervisor meant when he told me they hadn't figured out Phase 2. The founders of Kozmo had no idea how to turn a website, a warehouse full of food, and an army of bike messengers into a profit.

While it was satirizing social commentary then, the lesson of the gnomes are still echoed for many bike retailers today. Often times an owner or manager will come to the realization that they have been doing something just for the sake of doing it. Because that's the way it has always been done. Some examples of the underpants gnome's business model in bike retail today:

Phase 1: Sponsor a cycling club
Phase 2: ?
Phase 3: Profit

Nearly every bike retailer in North America has sponsored a local cycling club and on the surface it seems like a great investment. The store provides products or services at a discount to gain favor with the club and the people they influence. The trouble is the club and retailer have conflicting goals. The retailer's goal is to acquire new customers who are willing to pay full price for product, the club's goal is to acquire new club members who receive the discount or shop deal.

To make it worse the club spends most of their time either at their own events or at events with other sponsored clubs. The club calendar just doesn't make a lot of room for finding new cyclists and bringing them to the IBRs front door. Calling this "sponsorship" is incorrect; most retailers should instead call it "charity".

To truly be a sponsorship the club must have goals set by the IBR that funds it. Those goals can be free advertising (a logo on a jersey is not advertising), community service (trail building, clinics, kids' biking days), or a straight trade for something more concrete (each club member works 10 volunteer hours at the store). This would be an effective way to move from phase 1 to 3.

Phase 1: Start a Facebook page
Phase 2: ?
Phase 3: Profit

Everyone is on Facebook, at the time of this writing Facebook is in many ways the new Yellow Pages. Like the Yellow Pages a retailer will place an ad, it gets pushed out into the world, and hopefully someone finds that ad and begins a conversation. Instead of placing information in the Yellow Pages once a year a retailer will have to place information on Facebook 2-4 times a day. It can be a lot of work and if they're not careful it can be fruitless work that never leads to profit.

Luckily Facebook has a well-structured back end that can record reach, engagement, and even conversion when advertising on the platform. Though if a store manager is simply going on to Facebook 2-3 times a week and posting photos of whatever happens to be on sale, she may not be seeing the results she hoped for. I will break down more Phase 2 actions for Facebook in a later chapter.

Phase 1: Place a preseason order
Phase 2: ?
Phase 3: Profit

Even something like placing a preseason order can be lost in the confusion of phase 2. Many owners will tell me that phase 2 is "sell the product" but they're only partially correct. Many don't consider all the steps that have to be taken in order to sell the bike.

Vendors will approach the buyer for an IBR with numbers from the previous year and a request to increase the purchase by another 5-10 percent. This would be fine if the retailer had a forecasted plan for how they were going to market, promote, merchandise, and sell everything they're ordering. If not, then they're essentially ordering blind with the hope that people will walk into the door and want the things that just so happened to have been ordered.

In South Park, phase 2 symbolizes the actions someone is planning to take and how they will turn their tasks into a profit center. In this chapter we will focus on some of the most important aspects of bike retail: pricing, discounting, and running a Pareto analysis.

Wanamaker's Fair Pricing Plan

Pricing in an IBR, or in any retail for that matter, is dictated or heavily influenced by the manufacturer of the products they sell. Known as the List Price, Manufacturer Advertised Price (MAP) or the Manufacturer Suggested Retail Price (MSRP). The price dictated and advertised by the manufacturer is there to provide information to the consumer on what is believed to be a fair price. Many bike retailers will sell products below the MAP in order to move inventory and there are even some who could get away with selling the products for above MAP.

Working in a business where the price of the products sold is not set by the person selling them, it becomes a balancing act. A bike retailer will carry the products from several different brands in hopes to draw customers to their door. Meanwhile if other IBRs are selling the same products for the same price or less, a retailer will have to demonstrate a higher value proposition by offering a better location, better customer service, or a unique shopping experience; none of which are without extra cost to the business. Therein lies the balancing act, how does an IBR increase value while maintaining a price that has been determined by someone else?

Arguably the first person to ever combine bicycle sales with shrewd retail savvy was John Wanamaker. Wanamaker was a merchant who lived from 1838 to 1922. Along with being a retailer he was a religious leader, political figure, a pioneer in marketing, and considered by some to be the father of modern advertising. He was born and for most of his life lived in Philadelphia. He has been credited as the first person to ever take out a half and full page ad in a newspaper and the first retail merchant to hire a full time copywriter. While he sold nearly everything such as furniture, clothing, and tools he was also one of the largest bike retailers in the United States at the time.[3]

One of his more notable achievements was being the first major merchant to offer a return policy and establishing the common use of the price tag. Before Wanamaker, prices were constantly changing depending on a number of factors. If the product was in high demand, the price went up. If the store was busy, the price went up. If you were not a regular customer, the price went up. If you were only buying one instead of two, the price went up. If the store owner was having a rough day or just didn't like you, the price went up. Many customers saw this as an unfair system while the retailers saw it as smart business. In the mind of the retailer, if demand or costs go up then price should go up as well.

Wanamaker had a vision that all shoppers get treated equally and fairly. To do this Wanamaker introduced the price tag. He believed that there should be one price, all the time, no matter who they were or how often they shopped there. This simple strategy won over customers by the thousands and further established Wanamaker as one of the nation's best retailers.

The Wanamaker Store.

Interest Centers To=day in Bicycles

OUR fifth floor has been turned into a bicycle store with unique features. You will find it both an interesting and a luxurious place to visit.

On the 10th street side is the Bicycle Parlor and the Visitor's Pavilion. On the 9th street side is the Bicycle Track, embowered in palms and flowers.

For the next two weeks this programme will be followed:

Music on the Bicycle Floor, 10 A. M. to 5 P. M.

Fancy riding by a famous professional, every hour from 10 to 12 and 2 to 5.

Hourly spins by the Automobile Tricycle.

Exhibition riding by experts of both sexes on single wheels and tandems,—object lessons in bicycle-dress and bicycle "form."

CONCERNING the wheels we offer the public for the season of 1898, we believe our line one which combines in the highest degree those two irreconcilable elements, high quality and

Fig 2.2: An advertisement for bicycles from The Wanamaker Store in 1898. Retail experience and education of the sport were just as important to Wanamaker as price.

While the price tag is still alive and healthy today, we have never let go of the idea of a marketplace where price tags don't exist. Customers feel they deserve both a fair price and better pricing if they have demonstrated their willingness to dedicate themselves in some way to the IBR. Wanamaker's price tag, as it turns out, is a facade. The bike industry has never let go of negotiable or moving pricing structures. Manufacturers offer better terms and pricing based on the volume and inventory purchased. Thousands of retailers will offer different pricing to their customers depending on their amount of purchase, frequency of purchase, or loyalty to the store. Peter Fader may have said it best, "Charging everyone the same thing and treating everyone the same way, as retailers do today, is 'Six Sigma' thinking which is great for producing widgets on a production line, but it makes no sense in a world where customers are inherently different."[4]

IBRs have built dozens of systems that allow us moveable price tag. Frequent buyer programs, club memberships, buy two get one free, discounted tune-ups in the winter, or buy a bike and get

10% off of accessories. All of these are strategies to relive the glory days of the early 1800s when price tags did not exist.

What is Pricing?

Pricing can spark some of the most passionate conversations. Retailers never believe their margin is high enough, consumers never believe their cost is low enough, and manufacturers are hit from both sides as they try to choose the perfect MAP that will be competitive in the market without offending anyone. A price can evoke fear or pleasure, it can move someone to act or avoid, and it can inspire people to save or spend. Behind all the branding, the marketing, the advertising, and the sales pitches- the price tag is speaking the common language. So, when asked to best describe pricing strategies I always begin with the question, "What is pricing anyway?"

Pricing is powerful. Anyone who has ever worked in an IBR has surely bumped into a customer who is absolutely flabbergasted by the price of a bicycle. They blurt out, "How much?! For a bicycle?!" and they chuckle as they walk out the door sure to tell their spouse and friends that they saw a bicycle that cost a thousand dollars. Meanwhile Timmy is feeling very thankful that he didn't show them the bike that cost fifteen thousand.

Pricing is grading. Every year a new bike takes the mantle as the most expensive bike ever and we can all be assured that somewhere, someone bought it and took it home. Did they buy it because they felt that with great price comes great value? Probably not, it would be better to say "with great price comes great prestige". A $50,000 watch does not tell the time any better than a $5 watch. What a $50,000 watch does do is imply to everyone that the owner is a person of wealth, influence, and capability. A ten, fifteen, twenty, or even hundred thousand dollar bike can do the same.

Pricing is customizable. Every bike retailer has a customer or group of customers who get a deal that is a little bit different than everyone else. Pricing can be moved up or down depending on the person buying, the time of year they're buying in, or if they happen to be purchasing that bike that has been sitting in the rack for the past three years.

Pricing is secret. Everyone will hold their wholesale catalog close to the chest, fearful that if any customer (or even employee) ever saw it they would be held to the stake and proclaimed a rip off, a leech, someone who does not pass on the savings to the customer.

Pricing is instantaneous. Many customers will walk down an aisle of bikes looking at only the price tags. They continue walking until they see a price they are comfortable with only to realize they ended up looking at kid's bikes. Price creates an instantaneous response, those customers may have passed twenty bikes that would have suited their needs perfectly but price drove them away in a millisecond. Is the price right for me? Yes or no? If not, I'm moving on.

Pricing is a process. With every price tag comes a list of features and benefits and a list of reasons why that retailer believes that they are the ones to buy from. At the same time the customer has assigned a dollar value to all of these metrics as well. When the retailer's perceived value is higher than the customer's then the sales process begins.

Pricing is quantitative. Price will give people an idea of how many they should get, how many miles it should last, how soon before it needs to be replaced, and how much service it will require.

Pricing is qualitative. Price will give people an idea of where it was made, who designed it, who built it, and what it was made of. People will rightfully believe that the higher the price is the more skilled the craftsman, the more complex the design, the better the materials, and the better the service they should receive.

Pricing is risky. Every bike shop owner has wiped plenty of sweat from their brow over the most expensive bike on the floor. Did they make the right choice bringing the bike in? Will there be a customer who wants it and will it fit them when they do?

Pricing is never perfect. Every year the same conversations come up. How can we spend less and earn more? How can we convince our customers to buy at a higher rate? How can we convince our suppliers to sell at a lower rate? The needle is always moving, never still.

Pricing is drawing a line in the sand. Once a price is set a line has been drawn in the sand. Maintaining that line determines the health of the business. Maintaining that line puts food on the table, keeps the staff employed, and pays the rent through the winter. It's the nonverbal way to tell customers, "This is the value of this product when it is sold from this store. This is what we deserve and this defines our business' reason for being." If it budges, if it moves, it can leave an uneasy feeling for the retailer, like they've given up on something or someone.

It is difficult to define pricing because everyone has a different view and everyone responds differently. When it comes to pricing in bike retail the best owners understand all the things pricing can be and understand how to use pricing to their advantage when the time is right. When the time isn't right, these owners understand how to mitigate the negative effects.

Discounting and Sales

Jane goes into her local bike shop and starts shopping for a bike. She talks with Timmy who asks her questions about where she will be riding and then explains the features and benefits of a few models. Timmy and Jane communicate with each other very well, and they can both tell this is going to be a great retailer-customer relationship. Jane picks a bike she likes and is curious if the price listed is the best price available. Timmy offers her a discount and she agrees to buy the bike.

This story is being retold every minute in IBRs all over the world. Both Jane and Timmy have achieved what they hoped for. The question I like to ask is what happens next? When Jane talks to her friend Jim about her new bike what is she likely to tell him? Will she tell him about the quality of the bike and the all the great help that Timmy provided? Or will Jane tell Jim about the great price that she got? Jane will absolutely tell Jim about the discount. If she didn't tell him, she wouldn't be a good friend.

51

So Jim makes his way down to the bike shop and says, "My friend Jane bought a bike here and I was hoping I could get the same discount she got." And the cycle begins, Timmy is now known as a discounter. Jane tells Jim, Jim tells John, John tells Julie, Julie tell Jack, and so on. When a retailer starts discounting products it can be very difficult to stop.

In bike retail, price is a direct reflection of the value offered. To maintain higher prices retailers will have to be adept at selling value just as much as selling technical features and performance benefits. Discounts will erode one's ability to do that. Once an item is sold for a discount, the customer has been trained to focus on the price and it will be very difficult to switch the conversation back to the value that is being offered.

In his book The Power of Habit: Why We Do What We Do in Life and Business, Charles Duhigg discusses the structure of habitual behaviors. He teaches that every habit has three primary elements; cue, routine, and reward. The cue is the trigger that sets us down a path of habitual behavior, the routine is the repetitive action we make, and the reward is the comfort, pride, or achievement which validates the entire process.[5] For example when we wake up in the morning we are groggy (cue) so we stumble into the kitchen and make ourselves a coffee (routine) and after a cup or two we no longer feel groggy (reward).

In the short term all habitual behavior has a positive reward. In the long term, some habits can be very damaging and there is no better example of this in the bike industry than the habit of discounting. The vast majority of retailers I work with tell me their desires to stop discounting. They describe how it devalues the products they sell, how it is disrespectful to their skillsets, how it erodes the margins, how it limits the growth potential, and how it destroys the business from within. Yet despite this understanding many retailers still discount on a daily basis.

If retailers hate discounting so much, why do they still do it? I believe that discounting is no longer a choice we make, but a habit we have created. Discounting is a habit that we perform consistently and a habit that our customers have come to expect from us. Using Duhigg's framework, I will breakdown the habit of discounting by defining the cues, routines, and rewards that many IBRs are experiencing.

Cue: Customer asks for a discount on a bike.
Routine: Timmy discounts the bike 10%.
Reward: Timmy has sold a bike and gained some customer loyalty.

This is the most common habit of discounting. Many customers are trained to ask for a better price. Despite popular belief, they are in no way being disrespectful to person helping them, the business, or the value of the product. Asking for a better price is what smart consumers do. Where bike retailers can go wrong is with routine responses that give permission for the discount to happen. How can retailers change their routine but still achieve their reward?

Most people do not ask for a discount at Target, Lululemon, or the grocery store. These businesses have established a system to manage price conscious shoppers. They offer discounted products in select areas of the store, they advertise sales on old inventory, they have frequent buyer programs, and most powerfully- when a customer asks for a discount on product that is not on sale the answer is a very firm no.

When a retailer discounts a product they are not creating customer loyalty, instead they are creating price loyalty. Timmy's routine should have been this:

Cue: Customer asks for a discount on a bike.
Routine: Timmy says, "As it turns out we cannot discount this product but I can show you models from last year which are on sale."
Reward: Timmy has sold a bike and truly gained some customer loyalty.

For some IBRs this strategy will result in a handful of customers who choose not to make the purchase. Making the switch from a business known for discounting to a bike retailer that doesn't discount can cause some customer carnage. When retailers do this they are often surprised to learn that their best customers were never loyal them, rather they were loyal to the price. These same retailers however have found that customers willing to pay the MAP will offset the loss of price conscious customers.

Another example of a habitual discount is when Timmy learns that a competitor is offering to sell the same product for less. It plays out like this.

Cue: Customer mentions the bike shop down the street is selling the same bike for 10% less.
Routine: Timmy matches the competitor's price.
Reward: Timmy has sold a bike and demonstrated that he is competitive in the marketplace.

Retailers will often put the blame on the manufacturers for allowing other retailers to discount below MAP. They call up their sales rep and complain about the guy down the street selling the bike for 10% below MAP and give them a convincing argument for why the brand should be pulled from their store. It's a valid argument.

However I like to take a different viewpoint and ask retailers to imagine a hypothetical scenario where no bike brands in the world provide an MAP. That means every bike retailer purchases the bike for the wholesale price but are free to price the bike at any amount they would like. If this were to happen, what would bikes be priced at? Which retailers would aim for a 35% mark up and which would go even higher? Maybe 50% mark up or even a 100%? The bike shop down the street is obviously going to go the route of selling it for cheaper, which is the game they prefer to play. If any retailer believes they can sell the bike for higher amount than any of their competitors, I would ask why? What makes them so special, unique, and awesome to demand a higher price?

Differentiation is key to this scenario. To change this routine a retailer will have to find what their true differentiator is and stand firm that it is worth paying extra. There are many ways to be competitive in the marketplace. Doing it by price is a nonstop spiral to the bottom.

Here's another common discounting habit I run across:

Cue: Timmy believes the bike is too expensive.
Routine: Gives customers a discount without them asking
Reward: The bike is sold and Timmy feels better about himself.

This is one of the more frustrating scenarios I see. Timmy will often offer the discount even when the customer doesn't ask for it. He will say something like, "This bike is $2500 but I could sell it to you for $2250." In Timmy's mind this is a brilliant sales technique, he can demonstrate enormous financial value up front and the customer is bound to say yes, right? Wrong. In reality, this backfires in a monstrous way. If Timmy will cut 10% off a bike without the customer asking it will appear that all of the products are overpriced and Timmy is a deceptive, sleazy, price-gouging retailer.

If Timmy truly believes the product is too expensive then he needs more product training. If he is not confident enough to sell the product without discounting it then he needs more sales training. If it is absolutely impossible for Timmy to overcome these hurdles then it may be time to find him different tasks to do.

The last discounting habit is almost always done by the owner or manager of the store and touches on their confidence in the products they have selected to stock. It can be very worrisome to look at a $10,000 bike that has been sitting on the retail floor for two months. Did they make the right choice by buying this bike? Do they have a customer that will buy it? How will they pay it off if it doesn't sell before the bill is due? These are the questions running through every retailer's mind and this is how the habit of discounting plays out.

Cue: The manager is not confident the bike will sell
Routine: The bike is discounted.
Reward: The bike has sold and the manager has been reaffirmed he made the right choice by stocking that bike.

Managers have to set the example to Timmy. If the manager is willing to discount to win the sale, then Timmy will do exactly the same. If the product is not moving fast enough (and it is still before its turn date) then I would encourage managers to place more marketing behind it, remerchandise it, and make phone calls to customers who might like to take it for a test ride. As bikes get more expensive the potential customer base gets smaller, if retailers want to sell five-figure bikes they need to be prepared for the extra work to get it done.

To successfully change the habits of discounting it may require that managers train Timmy on the negative effects. Habits can be difficult to change so Timmy may need a better understanding of how his actions affect the bottom line. This may require managers to be more open with the books and the costs the business incurs. By doing this, Timmy is more likely to jump on board and work towards changing his routines.

In most stores Timmy knows the wholesale value of the bikes being sold. He learned this when he went to make his first employee purchase, through conversations he has had with coworkers, or perhaps he learned it because there is open access to all the pricing forms from the vendors.

When Timmy gives a customer a 10% discount on a bike he is usually comparing that discount to the wholesale cost and not the complete costs of running a business. It is helpful to sit down with Timmy and explain the costs of the business and how discounting will hurt him in the long run. This means teaching him about wholesale pricing, costs of labor, operational expenses, capital expenses, and any other costs the bike shop incurs. For example:

	$1000 Bike	$100 Jersey	$100 Repair
Wholesale cost	60%	50%	0
Labor cost	17%	17%	17%
Rent or mortgage	6%	6%	6%
Operational expenses	5%	5%	5%
Capital expenses	4%	4%	4%
Marketing expenses	3%	3%	3%
Profit	$50	$24	$65
Profit after 10% discount	-$50	$14	$55

Fig 2.3: Detailing where money is spent in the business and the effect of discounting. Your totals may vary.

In this scenario the costs equal $950 on a $1000 bike, meaning that the profit will only be $50. Unless Timmy decides to give a 10% discount, at which point the business will lose money. When the business loses money through discounting they have a couple of choices, first they either increase the number of sales that are not discounted. In this scenario, for every $1000 bike Timmy discounts, Timmy would have to sell two more $1000 bikes at full price to equal the same growth. The second choice is to cut back on expenses to better afford the discounts they're giving. That generally means fewer hours for Timmy or, in bad cases, Timmy gets laid off.

It is worth noting that there is a difference between discounting and putting products on sale. A sale is a systematic approach to moving old product while a discount could be offered to anyone at any time. Sales are healthy, discounts are not. Putting a product on sale is usually reserved for products that have either past their ideal turn rates, have been discontinued, or have been eclipsed by newer technology.

Once a product has passed its turn rate then the business is effectively losing money each week it stays in stock (If you do not know what a turn rate I won't bore you with the math here, just Google it). I recommend discounting these products by creating three levels of sale prices. One example:

- Level 1 Sale Price: 5% off MAP
- Level 2 Sale Price: 15% off MAP
- Level 3 Sale Price: Wholesale + 5%

Level 1 sale prices are reserved for the first two to six months after the product has passed its ideal turn rate. Level 2 is used when Level 1 sale prices have not been effective in moving the product and can be held for up to a year after the product was initially put into stock. Level 3 sale prices are used when the product has passed a year since it was put into stock.

Another reason to put something on sale is because it has been discontinued. In this case it is important to first assess the value of having "one of the last ever made". If a manufacturer decides to discontinue a very popular color, it might be worth keeping the MAP in place and promoting that it is the last of its kind.

If the product has been eclipsed by newer technology the need to put it on sale varies depending on the consumer demand for what is new. A $20 glove that is being replaced by a new model may not require the same percentage of discount as a $10,000 bike that is being replaced by its lighter, faster, and more innovative successor. In these scenarios retailers should be careful not to discount so low that it disrupts full MAP sales of bikes at a lower price range.

Switching the Focus from Price

People are trained to hunt for the best price, emboldened with the confidence to ask for the discount, and equipped with prices from competitors and in some cases, the manufacturers. Retailers should have a goal to move people away from price-focused shopping. One way to get people to stop focusing on the price is to have them focus on what the price gets them; the benefits of the product. This is a more advance set of retail skills but when performed well they can be very effective.

The first is to switch focus from the price to value by segmenting the product into its unique components. For many of the products and services retailers sell the sum may be greater than its parts. If a repair service is offered for $100, retailers may consider breaking down what each service and part would cost individually. When purchasing a package if a consumer is shown a savings over à la carte options people may see the value and tend to buy up. This same strategy can work for several of the bikes sold. Often the frameset, wheels, components, and assembly charges to build a bike from the ground up will be more expensive than buying a complete bike. Pointing to these individual costs can make a manufacturers retail price seem like a bargain, possibly blunting requests for a discount.

Another way is to redefine the value that someone is getting from a purchase. In the auto industry, Michelin tires have succeeded well with this idea. While the technology in each tire is loaded with features and benefits, it's difficult to show because every tire looks nearly identical; an enormous piece of rubber yanked from a mold. So Michelin changed the metric the consumer focuses on. Instead of features like siping or circumferential grooves, Michelin scores tires on a scale of 1-10 on wear life, braking, and comfort. Now, instead of paying $500 for high tensile steel belts, consumers are paying $500 for 20,000 more miles.[6] This metric resonates far better with their key customers.

In an IBR this could be used on the retail floor in a number of ways. Most manufacturers provide testing of their products, all the retailer has to do is tie these test results to a rider benefit that cannot be quantified in dollars, "This helmet weighs 30 less grams which means your neck will not be as sore." To the customer, what is the dollar value of 30 grams versus the dollar value of not having any neck pain? Or instead of telling people what adjustments are performed in a tune-up, a retailer can tell customers how long the service being performed will last. For example, "$30 guarantees service for 1 month, $60 for 6 months, and $100 for one year".

When a retailer can change to basis of the pricing structure or they can help move their customer's focus from price, to value.

Pareto Analysis

I am often asked for help on product selection. What should a retailer stock? How much should they stock? When should they carry it? Since bike retail and consumer demand can drastically change depending on what part of the world we are in I cannot provide advice on any specific brand or model that will ensure success, but I can provide a couple of tools that might help.

The Pareto Principle, or the 80/20 rule, was developed by Vilfredo Pareto, an Italian economist who lived in the late 1800s and early 1900s.[7] Through his studies he discovered what is seen today as a no-brainer, that a large percentage of wealth was held by a small percentage of people. This discovery was later popularized into a simple business formula that states 80% of the results come from 20% of the effort put forth, hence the name of the 80/20 rule.

The 80/20 rule permeates every part of business. 80% of profit will come from 20% of the products offered. 80% of a technician's time is spent on 20% of the services offered. 80% of sales will be conducted by 20% of the employees. The percentages may not always be as clear cut as 80/20 but the idea that a large percentage of results come from a small percentage of work holds true.

Before retailers place an order it is a healthy exercise to run a Pareto analysis of the products they sell. This will help determine where to place focus. In Fig 2.4 we see a Pareto analysis for a bike retailer. It shows 82.7% of their profit comes from 4 of the 12 bicycle categories they sell. They earned $152,895 from the sale of 555 bikes and building and extra 189 bikes only earned $32,016 in profit. That is a difference of $275 profit per bike versus $169.

Bicycle Category	Units Sold	Profit	Cumulative Total	Cumulative Percent
Men's Road	199	$70,017	$70,017	37.9%
Men's MTN	109	$40,483	$110,500	59.8%
Men's Hybrid	132	$25,420	$135,920	73.5%
Women's Hybrid	115	$16,975	$152,895	82.7%
Women's Road	45	$13,764	$166,659	90.1%
Junior Boy's	75	$4,651	$171,310	92.6%
Commuter	15	$4,403	$175,713	95.0%
Women's MTN	11	$2,112	$177,825	96.2%
Cyclocross	5	$2,058	$179,883	97.3%
Junior Girls	27	$1,909	$181,792	98.3%
Triathlon	3	$1,804	$183,596	99.3%
Track	8	$1.315	$184,911	100%

Fig 2.4: A Pareto analysis from an independent bike retailer

From a Pareto analysis one can also determine how time is being spent. Assigning a time value to the bike building process would give an estimate of which categories use up the most of the technician's time.

A Pareto analysis will only show what has been sold, it is important to note that it will not provide insight to why those items sold. Building and stocking over 100 junior bikes may have hurt the ability to sell more road bikes or they could have been the reason road bikes were sold. This type of analysis will have to be done in every store as retailers work with their customers, learn their shopping habits, and determine what drives their purchasing.

Chapter 2
Vansevenant Checklist

How do you react to pricing when you shop? How do your customers react to your pricing?

Are there any products or services that would be bettered if they were bundled as a package?

Is there any product or service that should be redefined so people have a clearer vision of what they are purchasing?

Run a Pareto analysis on bikes. Consider a separate analysis for equipment and service.

3

Checklists, Scheduling, Hours, & Brown M&Ms

"Stop looking out, start looking in, be your own best friend."
-Van Halen

When speaking to a group of retailers one of my favorite things to ask is, "Raise your hand if you have another bike shop in town that does crappy work." No matter where I am in the world or what city the retailers are from, everyone in the room raises their hand. My follow-up question is, "How do you know they do crappy work?" Again, regardless of where they are from the answer is the same. They tell me that they know their competition provides lousy service because customers bring in bikes and regal them with horror stories from the other shop in town. This conversation plays out like a movie script in every lecture I've done. Despite the predictable answers these retailers are correct, every IBR has a group of customers who openly complain about the bike shop down the road, across town, or in the next city over.

As I was working in bike retail these stories were a pleasure to hear, I ate them up. Nothing felt better than hearing from my customers how much better I was than my competition. It was easy to develop an ego. The stories were so wonderful to hear that they even worked their way into my sales discussions with other customers. When someone would tell me that they've visited the other stores, I'd share a story about how poorly they treated someone else. On one occasion I was giving a customer my usual game day speech about other bike shops when she asked me a question that left me speechless. She asked, "If the service at the other bike shop is so bad, why are they still in business?" I had no answer, I shrugged my shoulders and a few minutes later she left. Most likely to head down to the other bike shop and buy a bike. It was a solid Timmy move on my part.

Her question taught me that retailers can't treat everyone horribly and expect to keep the bills paid. People have no patience for poor service and will move to another store in a heartbeat if the experience is guaranteed to be better. If I could meet that customer again today I would answer her questions like this, "The reason that the other bike retailer is still in business is because their happy customers will never walk into my store to tell me how happy they are." Only disgruntled shoppers move from one retailer to another and start talking about it. People who are satisfied with the service have no reason to shop anywhere else.

No bike shop is perfect. Sometimes customers have a bad hair day, sometimes Timmy is tired and irritable, sometimes the store is busy, and occasionally the perfect storm occurs and all the wrong buttons get pressed. Timmy says something out of context, the customer misunderstands, and in a blink of the eye they are furious. Quickly driving to the next store in town where they will tell everyone why working with Timmy was such a nightmare. Every IBR has disgruntled customers. It is a natural part of doing business. It is impossible to please everyone.

Or is it? There are plenty of companies larger than bike retailers that have a solid reputation for quality customer service. How do they do it? Do they have something special that most IBRs do not? The answer is yes, they do. They have processes and procedures.

As companies grow and more customers come through the doors the challenge of ensuring a positive experience becomes more complex. Processes and procedures help ensure a consistent and positive experience for everyone. A great story that illustrates the value of ensuring a positive experience is the story about Van Halen's lead singer David Lee Roth and why he would not allow brown M&Ms in his dressing room.

In the 1980s rock groups were known for outrageous clothing, big hair, drugs, loud music, sex, wild parties and the craziest backstage antics. The boys in Van Halen were no different. Roth had put a stipulation in the band's contract that before every show a bowl of M&Ms be placed backstage, with all the brown M&Ms removed. If Roth arrived at the arena and found brown M&Ms in the bowl he would, in his words, "ceremoniously and very theatrically destroy the dressing room." This acting out was touted by many as an insane demand of a power-mad celebrity who got his kicks when taking advantage of others. To the surprise of many it was instead an ingenious ruse. Roth explained in his memoir, Crazy from the Heat,

"Van Halen was the first band to take huge productions into tertiary, third-level markets. We'd pull up with nine eighteen-wheeler trucks, full of gear, where the standard was three trucks, max. And there were many, many technical errors — whether it was the girders couldn't support the weight, or the flooring would sink in, or the doors weren't big enough to move the gear through. The contract rider read like a version of the Chinese Yellow Pages because there was so much equipment, and so many human beings to make it function. So just as a little test, in the technical aspect of the rider, it would say 'Article 148: There will be fifteen amperage voltage sockets at twenty-foot spaces, evenly, providing nineteen amperes . . .' This kind of thing. And article number 126, in the middle of nowhere, was: 'There will be no brown M&M's in the backstage area, upon pain of forfeiture of the show, with full compensation.'"[1]

In a video interview Roth went on to explain what would happen if he discovered brown M&Ms in the bowl. "So, when I would walk backstage, if I saw a brown M&M in that bowl . . . well, line-check the entire production. Guaranteed you're going to arrive at a technical error. They didn't read the contract. Guaranteed you'd run into a problem. Sometimes that would threaten to just destroy the whole show. Something that was literally life-threatening."[2]

On the surface having no brown M&Ms was a story of rock and roll excess, underneath it was a cleverly simple checklist to ensure a consistent experience regardless of the challenges the production faced. We can all take a cue from Roth and Van Halen to never underestimate the value structure, process, and checklists can play in any operation. They don't have to be complex to be effective; they just have to be well thought out.

For a bike retailer I would ask what systems have they put in place? What tasks do they have Timmy do every day? In this chapter I will review the many ways we can easily add process and procedure to bike retail and ensure a positive customer experience.

Checklists

Many owners would be bettered if they understood that their time should not be spent on any task that earns the business money. If an IBR has learned how to make money from selling a product or service, that learning should be systematized and carried out by someone else. The owner's time would then be freed up to focus on the next source of revenue, business partnerships, and community relationships.

In bike retail the owners have a very vivid picture for how things should be done. They have been doing these tasks for years and are so good at them, they are practically instinctual. When owners ask Timmy to complete the same tasks however, it never turns out the way they would like. Timmy fumbles, he makes mistakes, and he takes far too long to get it done. He just doesn't have the years of experience that the owner has.

Providing a checklist of the tasks to be completed would remove a lot of the guess-work for Timmy, will give him greater odds for success, and will speed up the training process. When an owner or manager has a lot to get done, providing checklists to the staff is a way to guarantee a consistent quality of work. Below

I will run through the most common questions and complaints bike retailers have about checklists.

Checklists are boring. Yes they are. In his book Checklist Manifesto, author Atul Gawande addresses how most people respond to checklists, "We don't like checklists. They can be painstaking. They're not much fun." Gawande goes on to say, "It runs counter to deeply held beliefs about how the truly great among us-those we aspire to be-handle situations of high stakes and complexity. The truly great are daring. They improvise. They do not have protocols and checklists."[3]

Before someone goes into a surgery the World Health Organization (WHO) requires the surgeon, nurses, and anesthesiologists to run through the WHO surgical safety checklist.[4] The checklist will ask questions regarding the site of the incision, if the patient has been given antibiotics, or if there are any risks that may present problems during surgery. Having gone through the checklists thousands of times, these are the questions that a trained surgery team has completely memorized. Since they have the checklists locked into memory, I am confident that many of them find the checklist tedious, boring, and in some cases insulting to their intelligence.

However, if a patient were about to receive surgery, would they want the surgical team to run through the checklist? Of course they would. That is because the WHO checklist isn't designed for the nurses' and doctors' comfort — the checklist is designed to ensure the patient has a consistent and positive experience.

Checklists are for important stuff, not small stuff. Many retailers can tell a story of when they showed up for work in the morning, prepped the workbenches, turned on the lights, started the televisions, and checked in the inventory only to realize that they had been "open" for two hours but never unlocked the front door. Humans are fallible; we will all forget something which is why even the small stuff deserves to be on a checklist.

Checklists take too much time. A great checklist is not a training manual. A checklist is not the place to be providing step-by-step instructions on a task. A well written checklist will say "1. Lights", it should not have eighteen sentences on how lights work.

I recommend keeping each line of a checklist under five words if possible, using simple questions or directions.

Timmy won't use the checklists. Handing someone a checklist without explaining why can come off as distrust. I would discourage managers from building checklists. Instead, I recommend having Timmy build the checklists and the manager add or remove what they see fit, and then approve them. This gives Timmy ownership over the tasks that need to be completed and with that ownership he will be more likely to perform the duties on the checklist.

If checklists can help surgeons in dozens of countries perform surgeries, then they can help bike retailers perform everyday tasks. Checklists are cheap- if not free, effective, and have a great return on investment, or ROI. Though the benefits don't stop at executing a procedure, a checklist allows one to be a more effective manager as well.

Many bike retailers in the world are above a snow belt, meaning that for several months of the year their community is buried under a blanket of snow. While there are always a handful of cyclists who ride through the winter for many retailers this weather means the day-to-day business of the store slows drastically. In many cases the revenue earned during the summer months needs to be more than enough to float the business through the winter. To maximize the health of the business many bike retailers are forced to use seasonal help. Seasonal help is a person or group of people who will start working in April or May and will leave in September or October (vice versa for countries in the southern hemisphere).

Seasonal employees are healthy for the business because they lower the overall labor costs. However seasonal help can be detrimental to the business because they require the management to retrain a new group of employees every spring. In many IBRs this training is pretty lackluster. I have seen some owners hire Timmy, hand him a pile of manufacturer catalogs, ask him to read through them, and expect that the next day he will be able to perform in the exact same manner as someone who has been working full time in the store for the past few years. If seasonal help is not provided with a thorough training plan it can be months of poor sales and damaged customer relationships before they are confident to work within the business.

When used as a training tool, checklists can get seasonal help up and running in a quarter of the time. On the first day the manager can walk Timmy through the store opening checklist, then on the second day they can hand Timmy the checklist and leave him to do the job by himself. Instead of Timmy attempting to read the managers mind, or trying to remember everything that needs to be done, Timmy can simply run through the checklist to ensure everything is done the way the manager would like it.

When Timmy learns and completes his checklists he has also demonstrated that he may be worth investment or offered more opportunities. Meaning checklists can double as performance reviews as well. Should Timmy fail to complete a checklist despite having been trained multiple times then it becomes easier for management when it comes time to offer (or not offer) Timmy more pay, benefits, or other opportunities.

As retailers begin to implement checklists in their business, I would discourage against any manager attempting to create checklists for everyone working. Handing a technician that has been working in the business for several years a new checklist can come off as controlling or dictatorial. Instead I teach managers to give employees the task of creating the checklists. For example, and manager can pull a technician aside and say, "You are the best at keeping your bench clean, would you create a checklist for all the other technicians to use?" This will empower employees to take the lead and increase the likelihood they will complete the checklists as well. The role of the manager is not to create the checklists, but to edit and approve as their employees create them.

I have compiled some common checklists that many bike retailers use.

Opening the store
Unlock doors and disarm alarm
Turn on lights, compressor, and displays
Turn on air conditioning or heat

Turn on computers and P.O.S. system
Run morning till procedures
Turn on music
Review notes left by closing staff
Clean parking lot, sidewalk, and entry way
Roll out outdoor displays, signage, merchandise, etc.
Clean countertops
Clean fitting rooms
Walk sales floor, restock as needed
Set up service area, restock as needed
Receive deliveries and update inventory
Call/text customers who need to pick up bike/deliveries
Answering machine to daytime message
Turn on open signs
Unlock doors

Closing the store
Announce closing 15 minutes prior to closing
Ensure all customers have left
Lock doors
Turn off open signs
Empty cardboard, garbage,
Cash out daily totals
Lock cash in safe
Answering machine to nighttime message
Return all tools
Sweep and/or vacuum
Clean all counter tops
Clean and stock restroom
Restock all missing bikes, equipment, and apparel
Post on communication board for morning staff
Turn off music
Turn off computers and P.O.S. system
Turn off air conditioning or heat
Turn off lights, compressor, and displays
Set alarm
Lock door

Midday restocking
Run a sales report
Confirm items in stock
Replenish stock as needed
Fold apparel
Set and face displays
Locate and schedule bikes to be built
Dust displays
Sweep
Inflate tires to ideal pressure
Set suspension sag for ideal test ride
Set saddle heights for best visual appearance

Many of the items on these lists could become checklists in themselves. Asking someone to clean and stock the restroom might sound vague. What needs to be restocked? How should they clean it? Should there be a separate checklist for each?

Remember that a checklist is not intended to replace an initial training; it is only a reminder of what needs to be accomplished. Managers should aim to train staff on what cleaning and restocking the restroom entails and if the staff are incapable of performing the tasks as they have been trained, it may require a more detailed checklist asking them to wipe down sink and toilet, sweep and mop floor, replenish towels and toilet paper, etcetera.

Hours of Operation

After a long and exhausting day at the bike shop many retailers just want to lock the door, turn off the lights, and relax their feet. However the customers just won't stop walking in. One after another asking, "Are you still open?" Those that have worked in bike retail know that turning away a customer is never the right choice, so they suck it up and get back to work.

When working with IBRs and discussing hours of operation for independent retailers, there is one question I ask. "Are your hours set for you or are they set for your customers?" When a bike shop has people walking in just before closing time, or a line of people waiting outside before the business is open, there is good reason to ask this question.

As a society, our workdays are getting longer and the ideal days of working 9-to-5 are all but gone. A recent study showed that 33% of people leave work between 5-6pm, 18% between 6-7pm, and another 18% leave after 7pm.[5] Add in a 30-40 commute and weekday shopping can begin as late at 8pm for some people. Large retailers like Safeway, Target, Wal-Mart have realized this and adjusted their hours accordingly. Opening earlier in the morning to catch people as they run quick errands before work and staying open well into the evening to be ready for their late night shopping needs.

Choosing hours of operations is based on a number of factors including the shopping preferences of customers, potential sales, and fixed costs of staying open. Managers also have to consider the willingness of their staff to work certain hours. Since cost of labor can range up to 20% of an IBR's total revenue it is crucial that every hour a store is open, it is open for a reason. Either to manage customer purchases or provide a customer service which creates profit later.

To help bike retailers make a more informed decision, in May of 2012 I conducted a study that took a closer look at hours of operations for IBRs in the United States. I sampled hours from a hundred bike retailers from 17 cities in the continental United States and compared them to a hundred other sporting goods retailers in the same cities.

Fig 3.1: Cities sampled: Los Angeles, San Francisco, Seattle, Salt Lake City, Tucson, Denver, Minneapolis, Des Moines, Kansas City, Oklahoma City, Austin, Chicago, Philadelphia, New York, Asheville, Atlanta, and Miami

The IBRs used in the study were an equal sampling of small, medium, and large stores. As well as a balance of branded concept stores versus more niche retailers.[6] The sporting goods retailers used were REI, Lululemon, Scheels, Northface, and Sportmart. These retailers were selected because they were seen as most likely to cater to past, present, or future customers for IBRs. They also have a great understanding of their financials and will study a market thoroughly when choosing their hours of operation. Essentially, bike retailers can take all the hard work done by chain sporting goods retailers and put the lessons learned toward understanding their market better.

Sporting goods retailers open earlier and close later than bike retailers in nearly all cases studied. The most common hours for a bike shop are 10-7 on weekdays, 10-6 on Saturday, and closed on Sunday. For sporting goods retailers the hours were longer in every instance: 10-9 on weekdays, 9-9 on Saturday, and 10-7 on Sunday. This begs the question, are sporting goods retailers providing a better service or taking potential customers from bike retailers?

Bike Retail Hours of Operation											
M-F OPEN		M-F CLOSE		SAT OPEN		SAT CLOSE		SUN OPEN		SUN CLOSE	
7AM	2	4PM	0	7AM	0	4PM	4	7AM	0	3PM	2
8AM	1	5PM	3	8AM	3	5PM	25	8AM	2	4PM	13
9AM	15	6PM	28	9AM	23	6PM	55	9AM	0	5PM	36
10AM	63	7PM	51	10AM	63	7PM	14	10AM	18	6PM	16
11AM	16	8PM	14	11AM	8	8PM	1	11AM	14	7PM	1
12PM	3	9PM	4	12PM	2	9PM	0	12PM	29	8PM	0
1PM	0	10PM	0	1PM	0	10PM	0	1PM	5	9PM	0
CLOSED	0	CLOSED	0	CLOSED	1	CLOSED	1	CLOSED	32	CLOSED	32

Sporting Goods Retail Hours of Operation											
M-F OPEN		M-F CLOSE		SAT OPEN		SAT CLOSE		SUN OPEN		SUN CLOSE	
7AM	0	4PM	0	7AM	2	4PM	0	7AM	0	3PM	0
8AM	11	5PM	0	8AM	11	5PM	0	8AM	4	4PM	0
9AM	18	6PM	0	9AM	59	6PM	6	9AM	17	5PM	3
10AM	68	7PM	3	10AM	22	7PM	21	10AM	34	6PM	22
11AM	3	8PM	14	11AM	5	8PM	29	11AM	24	7PM	46
12PM	0	9PM	76	12PM	1	9PM	42	12PM	10	8PM	18
1PM	0	10PM	7	1PM	0	10PM	2	1PM	0	9PM	0
CLOSED	0	CLOSED	0	CLOSED	0	CLOSED	0	CLOSED	11	CLOSED	11

  Median

Fig 3.2: Results of hours of operation study. 2012

With these results we learn that bike retailers are open 53 hours per week on average while sporting goods retailers are open 76 hours each week.

Opening earlier or closing later can prove fruitful though. Being the only bike retailer open in a city at 9pm might mean, over time, they will acquire new customers who would usually go to other stores but can't. If an IBR has a ride that leaves from their store every Saturday at 7am, earlier hours on Saturday would allow them to provide pre-ride services and sell products needed for the ride. These small gestures of good will go a long way. Mellow Johnny's in Austin, Texas opens their doors at 7am every day except Sunday when it opens at 8am. In a discussion with their manager I learned that business is generally slow in the morning. The customers that do stop by are generally dropping off their bike for repair before their workday begins and they are always grateful.

The study showed that Sunday was the most popular day for bike retailers to be closed with 32% locking the doors, compared to 11% of sporting goods retailers. If an IBR is choosing to close for moral or religious reasons, then by all means, I encourage them to do so. For other, smaller retailers closing down for one day a week may be helpful when attempting to save money. However, closing one day a week means being closed for 52 days a year, almost two months. Any retailer choosing to close one day each week will want to be absolutely sure they are making a smart financial decision.

If closing is essential to the stores health, I encourage retailers to choose the day they close very carefully. This means not relying solely on sales numbers but also measuring the amount of people coming through the door. If a store has people dropping off their bike for repair they might not be buying anything until a few days later when they pick it up and these types of customer services will not be seen on a standard sales report.

One extreme example of this can be found at Bike Fix in Rotorua, New Zealand where the nearby mountain bike trails attract visitors from all over the north and southern islands of the country. On weekends the influx of mountain biking tourists is so great that bike shops are significantly busier on Saturday than any weekday. Bike Fix chose to take this to the extreme and painting a huge sign across their front window reading, "Only Open Saturdays".[7] For Bike Fix, the cost analysis of staying open any other day was simply not worth it.

When setting hours of operation I like to ask two questions. First, are the hours set for the retailer's convenience or customers' convenience? Second, what are the hours compared to other sporting goods retailers in the area, and if they differ, why?

If any retailer were to choose to change their hours of operation they should not plan on seeing a drastic change for the first 3-6 months. Customers become trained to work around the set hours of the business, no matter how inconvenient. This is proven by how people work with banking institutions. Bank of America runs a tight ship in the US, closing on weekdays as early as 4:00pm in some cities. Meaning that if someone needed to get to a bank on a Tuesday, they'd likely have to use their lunch break or take time off of work. For most people, banker's hours are a complete hassle. If Bank of America changed their hours tomorrow and were open until 9:00pm, it would take a while before their customer base learned about the change. Those customers have been trained for years, and even decades, on what banker's hours were.

When an IBR changes hours they should plan on an increase in expenses while the customer base learns about the change. The process can be sped up with marketing efforts leading up to and after the change.

According to the study the most effective, and possibly lucrative, hours of operation for bike retailers would be 11-8 on weekdays and 8-6 on the weekends. Of course this can vary from one location to another and whatever the hours of operation are retailers would be wise to prove the effectiveness by measuring traffic flow and sales.

Scheduling

Once hours of operation have been determined the next step is to build the schedule for employees. Hours of operations are only the opening and closing times. They are not a sign of traffic volume throughout the day. To determine traffic volume IBRs should record what time of day transactions are at their highest; many point-of-sale systems, or POS systems, can do this. Once transaction volume is recorded the next step is to balance the productivity needs of the staff. Does the staff need time away from customers to perform repairs, merchandising, inventory, or cleaning? Once a retailer has this information they can build a schedule that leverages their staff while meeting their customers' needs.

Traffic volume. Bike retailers commonly experience two waves of traffic during a weekday. The first wave of traffic is over the lunch hour and the second wave is after 5pm. The lunchtime sales are predominantly smaller transactions. This could be someone picking up or dropping off a bike, grabbing some nutrition, or replacing their cleat. Customers visiting during the lunch hour simply do not have the time to hang out and talk about bikes. They get in, and they get out. After 5:00pm the sales require more time, more individual focus, and possibly more staff. This is when customers are more likely to consider purchasing a bike, have more questions, and more time to discuss the options of what to buy.

The weekends for most bike shops are as if someone turned on the faucet to full blast. Customers lined up before the stores opens and still lingering at closing time. This is why many bike retailers refuse to do appointment or scheduled work on the weekends, they are just too busy. The types of transactions on the weekend are all over the map. Small purchases, large purchases, bike drop off, bike pick up, and even customers who just want to hang out and talk. Anything can happen on a weekend.

For most retailers the plan of attack when it comes to scheduling is to arrive 20-30 minutes prior to opening and leave 20-30 after customers have left and the doors are locked. While there is nothing wrong with this, I will present some other options that may prove more efficient and offer greater customer service at the same time.

Scheduling technicians. How productive could a technician be with four hours of uninterrupted time? I have found that retailers who schedule technicians at hours when the store is not open have a higher volume of work done in a shorter amount of time. Having two technicians working from 7am to 10am, completely uninterrupted, can result in nearly doubling the output of the service area.

Scheduling leadouts. If opening procedures never seem to get done before customers begin flooding into the store, perhaps a retailer could combat this by scheduling a leadout to work before the store opens? This will allow him or her to manage deliveries, update inventory, merchandise the retail area, and complete anything else on the store opening checklist. Essentially, this person is there to prep the store for a day of business. All other leadouts could work during open hours.

Scheduling bike fitters. If a bike fitter working two hours will earn as much or more than a technician working the same amount of time. This could be motivation for having bike fitters working full time, just as technicians do. For many IBRs in the US the question, "Should we have a fit studio?" is a no brainer, now the question has moved to, "How many fitters can we have working at one time?"

I recommend to not schedule bike fitting before or after open hours. Bike fitting is a service but it is also a show. Performing a fit during open hours can help sell more fittings as customers see the service taking place.

Scheduling managers. I strongly encourage managers to be at the store when customers are, constantly ensuring the highest level of service for the people walking in. This does not mean that managers are working directly with customers, though they should if they are needed to. This means that managers are overseeing the technicians, leadouts, and bike fitters to ensure everyone is offering the best possible service.

Chapter 3
Vansevenant Checklist

Build checklists. Start by having your staff create the checklists, and then you edit and approve them. Here are some checklists you could start building:

Opening the store
Closing the store
Midday restocking
Managing warranties
Placing orders
Checking in a bike
Hiring process
Sales process

Are the hours of operation set for your convenience or the customers' convenience?

What are your hours compared to other sporting goods retailers in the area, and if they differ, why?

Build a schedule for technicians, leadouts, bike fitters, and managers that achieve both great customer service and high productivity. Consider the value of having people work when the store is not open.

4

The Timmy Factor

"Be a yardstick of quality. Some people aren't used to an environment where excellence is expected."
- Steve Jobs

During a discussion with IBR owners and managers in Melbourne, an industry veteran with over 20 years in the industry asked me "How do I get people to do what I want?" On the surface the question seems simple but like peeling an onion, it has layers. Ideas on employee motivation have filled thousands of articles, books, speeches, and workshops meanwhile the psychology of motivation is tremendously complex and any progress we have made in the past century has been quite small.

To better answer this question I refer to Dr. Susan Weinschenck for insights on how to persuade and motivate people. Weinschenck has a Ph.D. in Psychology and over thirty years of experience as a behavioral psychologist. Her clients call her "The Brain Lady" because she applies research on brain science to predict, understand, and explain what motivates people and how they behave. In her fourth book, How to Get People to Do Stuff, Weinschenck describes the seven drivers of human motivation.[1] They are 1) the need to belong, 2) habits, 3) the power of stories, 4) carrots and sticks, 5) instinct, 6) the desire for mastery, and 7) tricks of the mind. This is how they may take shape in a bike shop.

The need to belong. Humans are pack animals and rooted in our DNA we have a need to belong to something. This is why we have far more people looking for a cycling team, club, or group instead of taking on the sport of cycling solo. Employees also have this desire to belong to the group and a manager can leverage this as motivation. For example, when a manager asks someone to complete a task, instead of saying "Inflate all the tires" Weinschenck would suggest putting the request in context of the group. "Could you help us out by inflating the tires?" This way employees will see how their work is contributing to the group.

Habits. Just as we are pack animals, we are also creatures of habit. For example, I believe that people do not make a conscious decision to pour a cup of coffee in the morning. Instead they are habitually responding to their cue of morning grogginess by shuffling to the kitchen and, without any real memory of how they got there, pour a cup of coffee. Managers can leverage habitual behavior and even create habits for people. The easiest way to do this is by anchoring a new habit to an old one.

The power of stories. Ever notice how people never post Instagram photos of something boring? Instead they post photos of wonderful landscapes, travel, or intimate family moments. There are never images of people staring blankly into the television with potato chip crumbs on their chest. On Instagram a person's life is edited to appear exciting, unique, extraordinary, and productive.

If this is the story employees are telling other people they will continually look for opportunities to continue the narrative. Managers can leverage this by giving staff tasks that align with his self-personas. If their persona is that of an artist then a merchandising task may resonate with them. If they see themselves as clean and structured then a goal to organize a workbench may help them tell their story.

Carrots and sticks. Carrots are positive reinforcement, sticks are negative. This is the simplest form of employee motivation and one that many managers default to first. If people do something well, managers congratulate them or even present them with a gift; this is a carrot. If an employee does something poorly, a manager will have a discussion with them to show how they are letting down the team; this is a stick. It is not recommended to give entirely carrots or entirely sticks. A balance is what has been proven to work best.[2]

Instinct. Instinct is a huge motivator, especially instincts as they relate to loss. People are instinctually more motivated by losing something than by gaining something. The potential of losing hours, money, or even opportunities can all be motivators to achieve.

The desire for mastery. One thing more powerful than reward is an employee's own desire to master their skills and knowledge. However this does not always mean that managers should play the sage teacher, I would discourage standing over their shoulders while they build their first bike from the box. Instead give staff the autonomy to chase after mastery by presenting with the appropriate tools and teach them to ask questions when they are lost. The journey to discover and develop skills can be far more rewarding than having step-by-step instruction.

Tricks of the mind. Managers can use mind tricks to motivate their staff. For example, people are more likely to do something if they verbalize the situation as a question to themselves. An employee asking himself, "Why am I late for work?" is better than a manager asking "Why were you late for work?" So for managers it is important to inspire the internal questions rather than make statements. This takes time to build into the culture but when achieved can be very valuable.

To recap the seven drivers of human motivation are 1) the need to belong, 2) habits, 3) the power of stories, 4) carrots and sticks, 5) instinct, 6) the desire for mastery, and 7) tricks of the mind. An IBR owner or manager understands the psychology that is put in place they can leverage it to motivate and inspire.

I Don't Do It For The Money, But...

Everyone working in bike retail has a number; the amount they make per hour, their annual salary, or their commission rate. Everyone has a number and everyone wants their number to go up. I've had many retailers tell me they do the job because they love it, that money is not important. However, they are never comforted by the thought of earning less than they currently are. Regardless of how passionate someone is about working in bike retail the money is still important and everyone believes life could be nicer if their earnings were higher than they are.

A salary can be seen as one's potential and success in life. If someone makes enough money they are more comfortable at the thought of buying a home, getting married, having kids, or at the very least buying more bikes. As a manager in the business it is important to keep a pulse on how people feel about their earnings and recognize when they begin to feel undercompensated. There are many different ways an owner or manager could be paying their staff. For example:

1. Pay (hourly, salary, or commission)
2. Bonuses
3. Health benefits
4. Insurance
5. Paid time off
6. Paid sick days
7. Discounts on product / free product
8. Spiffs
9. Gifts
10. Paid entry fees to races
11. Paid education

Anything that would have cost someone money out of their pocket but the business paid for instead is a type of financial wealth. What is interesting about this list is that no matter how much an IBR invests in numbers 2 through 11, the people working will spend the majority of their time thinking about number 1;

their pay. They will be asking themselves constantly, "How much am I getting paid?" So let's drill down on the three most popular forms of paying people- hourly, salary, and commission.

Paying an hourly wage will help maintain lower labor costs in the business. An hourly wage allows most employers to forgo some additional costs like insurance and paid vacation, plus it often carries a different tax structure as well. Hourly pay is great for part-time staff, seasonal help, or anyone working on a trial period.

There are two big downsides to hourly pay, the first is overtime. Should anyone work over 40 hours in one seven day period the employer is required to pay time plus one-half of their regular rate. Why this is bad is because many employers struggle to keep track of how much someone has worked each week and risk going over budget.

The second downside to paying hourly is employees' tendency to have a lower morale, lower work ethic, and lower commitment to the job. This is because the math of hourly work is incredibly easy to do. If Timmy is making $8 per hour and spent one hour selling a bike for $1000, it's very easy for Timmy to do the math and come to the conclusion that he is undervalued. Hence, morale and motivation drops. An hourly rate is also a message of commitment from the employer. When management offers someone an annual salary they are verbally committing to the employee for a full year, offering an hourly wage means that they're commitment is on an hour-by-hour basis.[3] If management is not committed to Timmy, why should Timmy be committed to them?

Paying salary is great for full time employees and when done correctly, can be quite the carrot to strive for. For most employers, salary pay carries additional benefits like health insurance, paid time off, and paid sick days. Opposite to hourly pay managers can expect a salaried employee to have a longer term of commitment, higher morale, and a stronger work ethic.

The third type of pay, and the one that causes the most controversy, is commission. Commission based pay and bike retail are very old friends and there are many bike retailers in the world who are operating on a commission base pay structure. Rather than run through the pros and cons of commission based pay I want to share my favorite commission plan for paying employees.

1. Provide a salary or hourly wage to all employees that is a decent living wage.

2. Set sales goals and margin goals for every week of the year. Use the past three years as reference and add the ideal growth percentage. It is critical to have both sales and margin goals.

3. When staff break both the sales goal and the margin goal for the week give them a percentage of whatever amount is over that goal. It may be 5% pay out or it may be 100%, it doesn't matter because the goals of the business have already been met.

4. Split the commission based on hours worked. The people who worked the most hours will take home the largest percentage of the commission. Give all employees a piece of the commission, not just leadout on the retail floor. Owners and managers should not take a portion of the commission.

5. Create a weekly report showing everyone's individual sales and margin numbers, how the company is trending against previous weeks, and the goals for the following 2-3 weeks.

I prefer this structure because it promotes teamwork when helping customers, inspires everyone to think of themselves as a leadout (even technicians), and discourages discounting. However, since the structure is based on achieving sales and margin goals for the business everyone understands that if the store does not achieve its goal first, no one receives a commission.

This all leads to a big question, how much should an IBR pay their staff to begin with? Research of the US Department of Labor, Bureau of Labor Statistics website contains information for nearly 300,000 people working as "retail salespersons" in "sporting goods, hobby, and musical instrument stores". It shows an hourly median wage of $10.54 and an annual median wage of $21,920.[4]

One of my favorite phrases when it comes to determining pay for someone is, "If you pay peanuts you get monkeys", implying that only stupid people will choose to work for a retailer that does not offer a competitive and livable wage. Managers should be prepared to pay for the talents they need. A team filled with hard working and engaging leadouts, efficient and friendly technicians, and experience oriented bike fitters will take the business to outstanding heights, but it is not cheap.

In her TED talk, titled The Good Jobs Strategy, MIT Sloan School of Management Professor Zeynep Ton discusses the topic of pay for retail workers. She says, "The conventional wisdom is that this is how the world is supposed to work if you want low prices. If companies offered better jobs they would have to increase their prices or make less money. There is almost an assumed tradeoff between good jobs and low prices. But this is a false trade off because there are very successful companies operating right now that provide good jobs to their employees, low prices to their customers, and strong returns to their investors all at the same time."[5]

Ton goes on to detail components of this in her book Good Jobs Strategy[7] by showing examples of retailers who are successful by investing in labor. They do this by reducing costs by offering customers less, standardizing tasks while empowering employees to improve those standards, cross training, and operating with slack by erring on the side of overstaffing. To surmise, an IBR should strive to eliminate waste in everything but staffing. IBRs that invest in employees are by no means easygoing about what people do. Rather, they are obsessed with eliminating waste and improving efficiency.

To answer the question, how much should staff be paid? I believe retailers shouldn't pay them what they're worth today. They should pay them as if the business had already achieved its financial goals. Setting the stage for success is done by showing commitment to the staff.

Below I have detailed out 6 more ways IBRs can provide financial wealth to people.

Bonuses. My only rule with financial bonuses is that they are not given out on a schedule. When owners or managers give out an end-of-year bonus it is seen as a great reward the first year, a nice thing to have the second year, and then it is expected every year after that. I believe that bonuses are given when business goals are not just met, but are obliterated. Bonuses are given out when someone goes above and beyond the call of duty. Bonuses are rare gifts and when they are given they are a statement to someone's work ethic, work quality, and drive for success in the store. Bonuses should never be expected.

Discounts on product or free product. When someone asks Timmy what kind of bike he rides what should his answer to be? I would prefer his answer to be "I ride the best bike in the store." Here's why; to a customer, Timmy is the most knowledgeable person about bikes and he could ride anything in the store. If Timmy chose to ride a slapped-together klunker then in the customer's mind they may be buying beyond their needs. They may think, "If a slapped-together klunker is good enough for Timmy, who is a better and more committed cyclist than me, do I really need a $5000 bike?"

I encourage that every year all full time staff receive a brand new bike of their choice, as long as it is a current year model and the top of the line. Staff are required to ride the bike a minimum amount of miles each month (managers can use Strava.com to track their miles). At the end of the season sell the bike as used, recoup the wholesale value, and purchase each staff member a newer model. If Timmy crashes, damages, or breaks something on his bike he has to pay for the repair. This strategy is break-even for the shop but the return on the retail floor is enormous. With this gesture IBRs will have built a team of dedicated staff who can answer the question by saying, "I ride the best bike in the store and let me tell you why."

Spiffs. A spiff is an immediate bonus for achieving a goal, usually money. Every store has dogs sitting around; bikes that have been there for three seasons, a long sleeve jacket from a now defunct pro team, and a brand new tapered crankset. These are the items that are perfect for a spiff. Managers can offer a $25, $50, or $100 reward to the person who sells these products because they are losing money every day they stay in inventory. Some fun ways to do that is to ask staff to post the product on their social channels and write a creative advertisement for it. Managers can also challenge employees to find the most creative way to display it or present ideas on how to package the item with a group of products.

One of my favorite spiffs is a game I call "Sisterhood of The Travelling $100 Bill In My Pants" (awesome title, I know). When the first sale of day is made call a store meeting, gather everyone around and reward Timmy for the $12 inner tube sale he just made. The manager announces to everyone that they are rewarding Timmy with a $100 (best done with a clean $100 bill). They then tell everyone that the $100 can be taken from Timmy if they have a sale higher than his. The person at the end of the day with the highest sale will take home the $100. Let the race begin.

Gifts. Giving a gift is for very special occasions only. They are limited to holidays, birthdays, anniversaries, newborns, or as a very special show of gratitude. A gift should never be money- that's a bonus. A gift is a new set of tires, a dinner out with the spouse, or a gift card to their favorite non-cycling store.

It is important to note that the best gifts are not defined by how expensive or showy they are. A gift should be personal. If management gives a gift that the employee has no interest in then they are only showing how little they know about the people working for them.

Paid entry fees to races. Set an annual amount for race entry fees that anyone can use as they wish. Participating in events will get staff involved with the community and speaking to customers out in the wild. I would not limit it to just bike races. Running events, triathlons, duathlons, or adventure races are all fine. Any event where they are likely to talk to cyclists or people who have a high potential to become cyclists.

Managers do not need to require that their staff podium to receive the payback, though they may require their staff to finish the event. $100 to $150 a year is a good amount, with that they'll be able to do 4-6 mountain bike races or pay for 15% of an Ironman.

Paid education. Companies like Specialized, Park Tool, and SRAM offer educational courses for IBR staff.[7] This is not the type of education I'm referring to (though I do encourage managers to send their staff to these programs). I'm talking about helping someone earn a degree from an accredited college or university. Investing in someone's education shows commitment to their growth and in return they will show theirs. I would not require a payback if they fail a course, I would only require a payback if they drop out. It should be contracted that if they quit their job or are terminated before their courses end, payment for the education will stop.

IBR managers can use these strategies to develop a great balance of financial wealth in the business.

Be Nice

We've all had jerk-face bosses in our lives. People that treated us like inferiors, treated us as if we were dummies, yelled, ridiculed, and even harassed us. A positive work environment is key not just to employee morale and productivity but to providing quality customer service as well. Here are some of the best practices I've seen from bike shop owners and managers on how to create a positive working environment.

Regularly checking in. Once a month, invite people to sit down and talk. Ask them how they are doing and what they need help with. Having an open door policy isn't enough- invite them to the conversation.

Be open to criticism. Ask people for clear ideas on how to be a better manager. When they express ideas, do not be defesive. Truly consider doing it.

All ideas are valid. If a manager doesn't like an idea they should never criticize, instead tell the staff that they're off to an exciting start but would like to see more detail or a different direction.

Pizza night, free lunch, donuts for breakfast, or drinks at the end of a day. Nothing brings people together quite like food. And on a busy Saturday buying lunch for everyone will keep them in the store more to help customers.

Show gratitude. Studies have shown that saying thank you can inspire people to be more efficacious and make them feel more valued? I encourage managers to say thank you and say it often, but only if they're sincere. Managers shouldn't just say "thanks" but rather tell them why they're grateful for their work, for example, "Timmy, you really helped me out today by getting those bikes built. Thank you."

Get out of the way. Once a manager has given their employees a task, they should step aside and let them work. Constant interruptions and corrections do not show a sense of trust.

Notice that 5 of the 6 suggestions will not cost an IBR any money; they will only cost time and energy. Retailers can make incredible impacts without spending a cent.

A great manager cultivates positive relationships among the entire staff by building an environment where people are open to helping each other, push each other to achieve, and communicate effectively. Being nice is essential to cultivating relationships.

Clear Their Path

Timmy starts his day like any other. He grabs a stack of repair tickets, glances through them, and chooses his first project of the day. He's going to perform a fork service a bike cleaning, and a derailleur adjustment on a 2-year old Specialized Enduro.

Timmy spends the first twenty minutes looking through the back room. He has difficulty finding bikes when they are piled up on top of each other. Ten minutes go by before he finds the Enduro. He gets the bike in the stand and would set up his supplies but can't find the bucket to put on the floor underneath the fork. After another 30 minutes of searching, Timmy finds that someone used the bucket to collect trash in the back room. Now he has to walk the bucket out to the dumpster before he can start his work. More than an hour later, with the fork done Timmy starts the bike cleaning, but this bike is a mess. It has a dozen rides worth of dirt caked into the tires, the cassette looks like someone lubed it with motor oil, and the saddle has lines of salt from where the person riding it sweat through their shorts. So Timmy takes a deep breath and reaches for a few rags and a spray bottle. Lastly Timmy goes to adjust the brakes and derailleurs but can't find his Allen keys, another 15 minutes go by before he sees them being used in the fit studio.

Who can assign people to clean and organize the back room? Who has the authority to go out and buy enough buckets to do all the needed tasks? Who is responsible for investing in a parts washer or a bike washing bay? And who is going to approve an order for more tools in the fit studio? The owners and managers are.

Timmy may never know that there is an easier way to do his job, in his mind the way he works is the way it has always been done. If he is aware that the job could get done faster and with less hassle then odds are good he's annoyed that his managers haven't made the appropriate investment. I believe one of their most important tasks for managers IBRs is to provide the resources and tools their employees need to perform their job as efficiently and professionally as possible. Doing this is clearing the path for their employees.[8] To better spot these path-clearing opportunities I recommend the following:

Be aware. Look at the day to day tasks the staff is completing. What tasks take the longest? Is there is any way to make the task more efficient?

Have an open mind on ordering supplies. If someone wants to order a different chain lube, be open to it. Hear out their reasoning and make the best choice for the customers.

Provide a monthly budget for each employee to spend on supplies.

Run monthly tool checks to see what tools went missing or were broken. Replace what is needed.

Aprons, shirts, cleaners, mops, brooms, towels, trash bags, toilet paper, etcetera. Always keep a full stock of the items people will always need.

Research other bike shops. Learning a better way means seeing how other people get it done.

Training and Recruiting

If a manager has ever asked, "Who is the best person to hire?" they should also be asking, "What is my training plan for people I hire?" Recruiting and training are two weights on the same barbell. They are linked in every way.

At the home of the Big Mac, McDonalds, employee turnover rate is an astounding 150%.[9] This means that once the fry cook has served 8 months at a McDonalds, he has probably been there longer than anyone else he works with. To have a turnover rate this high means that McDonalds does not have the luxury to wait for dream candidates and is often forced to hire any warm body that walks through the door.

Since McDonalds will not have the luxury to be selective about whom they hire they must be very diligent in how they train. It is impossible for McDonalds to spend three months training someone when they are likely to leave just five months later. The training process at McDonalds has been relentlessly refined to achieve maximum results in minimal time. Everything in a McDonalds restaurant has been broken down to a systematic set of easy-to-follow procedures dubbed the McDonalds Gold Quality Standards.[10] Using this systemized training McDonalds can hire someone at 8:00am and have them assembling Big Macs before the lunch rush.

For IBRs, the worse the training processes are the more thorough and intense the recruitment processes should be, and vice versa. An amazing training plan provides the ability to hire people who may not already possess the specific skills needed to accomplish a task, broadens the scope for who can be hired, and provides the management leverage when it comes to offering pay and benefits.

Counter to that, a weak training process is not detrimental to a business. It just means the managers are more specific in their needs when interviewing people. They search longer and are prepared to pay accordingly when they find the right person.

Firing

Many bike retailers in the past have had to have an uneasy conversation. For retailers who are in this position, if this is a conversation that they're dreading, I fully understand. It's not easy, but when it happens and it is time for employees to move on to their next opportunity, the business will be stronger for it. Below I have listed the most common mistakes managers make when having this difficult conversation.

"This is really hard for me." When terminating someone they don't care how you feel. Addressing personal feelings is selfish and not going to make the conversation easier for anyone. Be polite but straightforward.

"We've decided to make a change." This is what to say in a press conference or when swapping riders in an off-season trade. Skip the platitudes. If managers have done their job right the employee knows this conversation was a possibility.

"We will work out some details later." Managers should have worked them out by now. Give them appropriate amount of time to collect their stuff, a date to have company property returned, and have any paperwork ready, especially severance pay. It is best to have this entire process planned or done before beginning the conversation.

"You just aren't cutting it compared to Timmy." When firing someone never compare them to someone else as justification. It turns something that was objective into a personal black hole that can never be escaped.

"Ok, let's talk about it." Most of the time people will sit there quietly, but a select few will want to argue. This can be very dangerous, have this phrase ready if you need it, "We can talk about this all you'd like but it will not change the decision I've made." If they start to vent it doesn't mean managers need to respond. Listening may be the best thing they can do.

"You do great work but we need to cut staff." When truly downsizing, which can be very typical for seasonal businesses, managers should just say so and leave performance out of it. If they're not really downsizing and just hiding behind it as an excuse they will appear as untrustworthy to the rest of the staff when the employee is replaced.

"You don't like it here and we both know you'll be happier somewhere else." They do not need anyone to point out the silver lining. They can do that on their own.

"I need to walk you out." Unless they're a criminal, don't treat them like one. Just give them a time frame to collect their things and a firm handshake before they go.

"We have decided to let you go." The best thing to do here is to take ownership, don't use the word "we" and instead say, "I have decided to let you go." Saying "we" can imply that everyone working there wanted them fired and that is just a mean idea to plant.

"If there is anything I can do, just let me know." Like what? Like giving them their job back? Like writing a letter of mediocre recommendation? Maybe calling the other bike shop and put in a good word? If an owner or manager can do anything it is in regards to final payments, 401k details, and other HR work.

Remember, that when it comes time to terminate someone, it is all about them.

Chapter 4
Vansevenant Checklist

What is the best way to motivate Timmy to go above and beyond?

What is your pay structure?

If you need your staff to do more or if you need more talented people, how will you pay them?

How can you increase the financial wealth of your staff? Bonuses, spiffs, commission, discounts to events, or education?

When someone asks Timmy what type of bike he rides, what will his answer be? Can you create a new bike program for your staff?

How can you be nice to your staff? How can you engage with them on a personal level?

Do you say thank you in a direct and meaningful way?

Be aware. Look at the day to day tasks your staff are completing. What tasks take the longest? Is there any way to make the task more efficient?

Have an open mind on ordering supplies. If someone wants to order a different chain lube, be open to it. Hear out their reasoning and make the best choice for your customers.

Can you provide a monthly budget for each employee to spend on supplies?

Start a process for running monthly tool checks to see what tools went missing or were broken. Replace what is needed.

Research other bike shops.

What is your current training process and can it be better? How?

Do you have someone who needs to be terminated? How will you go about moving them out of the business?

5

Managing Technicians

"I go as fast as I like. Street sign says one way east, I go west."
-Jack Casey, from the movie Quicksilver

The sketch begins with a man dressed as Superman, complete with the bright blue suit, red cape, and "S" across his chest. However the costume he is wearing looks second rate, as if it were a bottom-of-the-bin rental from a local costume shop. The entire suit has clearly been stuffed to beef up the chest, shoulders, and biceps. It makes people chuckle more than awe, but then again, that should be expected- this is a Monty Python skit after all.

As our Superman stands triumphant with his fists resting on his hips the narrator begins. "This man is no ordinary man. This is Mr. FG Superman. To all appearances, he looks like any other law-abiding citizen." As the camera backs out it becomes apparent that everyone in the city is dressed in the exact same costume. Now the stage is set, we are clearly living in a world of Supermen. The narrator continues, "But Mr FG Superman has a secret identity. When trouble strikes, at any time, at any place, he is ready to become... BICYCLE REPAIRMAN!"

Whether they knew it or not Monty Python were making an interesting bit of social commentary with the Bicycle Repairman sketch.[1] In a world of superheroes and unlimited powers, no one understands how to fix a bicycle. The sketch is art imitating life. Most people are more comfortable changing the tire on their car than on their bicycle. People can understand how to cook a five course gourmet meal, write code for a website, or install a home theater but the springs and lever systems of a rear derailleur are somehow baffling. The skillset that a bike technician has is one that is respected and valued by cyclists everywhere and we could all take a lesson from Monty Python and treat our services areas as the valued resources they are.

If Bicycle Repairman truly existed and all bikes were maintenance free from this day on. Many owners would have no problem shutting down the service area, filling it with bikes, and focusing all of their energy on selling rather than fixing. Bicycle service is often seen and treated as a necessary evil. This is proven by the lack of investment placed in service areas and the minimal attempts to grow the service side of the business despite it having the highest profit margin. Where a bicycle sale will bring 15% profit margin at a maximum, bicycle service will often earn 50% profit margin at a minimum. Sadly though, when it comes time to have a heart to heart discussion on expansion, investment, or how to grow the business- the conversations almost always involve more product on the retail floor.

In my work with retailers the average amount earned from service labor is only 6% of total revenue. The highest I have ever seen, meaning I saw the financial statements, was 13%. To reference Bicycle Retailer and Industry News once more, 11.4 percent of their revenue comes from repair parts and labor, compared to only 6.5 percent for the average. I believe that bike retailers will be forced to lean on their revenue from service as the primary income in their business. Fred Clements, the Executive Director of the National Bicycle Dealers Association has researched this subject and has said, "As internet sellers continue to challenge brick and mortar for product sales, some of the difference may be made up in an area where internet sellers find it difficult or impossible to compete." [2]

Saying that online retailers are challenging the brick and mortar model is an understatement, online retailers are completely uprooting and forever altering the way business will be done. One by one, every product a bike retailer sells will be competing with similar products online. Helmets, cycling shoes, apparel, components, and even a bike can all be purchased online. Someone can have everything they need to be a cyclist without ever stepping foot in an IBR. This uprooting and fundamental change in business has happened in nearly every industry, and it will happen in the cycling industry as well. It is just a matter of time.

For most bike retailers, the services they offer are the only sales they truly own. They've created the services, named them, and marketed them. Nearly every other item that is sold is an item where the IBR acts as a middleman between the manufacturer and consumer. This type of middleman role is becoming obsolete in many industries. In the future the services a bike retailer offers will be the safety net of the business and the primary revenue stream.

At the 2012 Bicycle Film Festival, Show Love presented a feature on 718 Cyclery in Brooklyn, New York.[3] The short film details the shop's process for selling and servicing bikes. In the film Joe Nocella says it best, "You can't hammer a nail over the internet. You can't be a butcher over the internet. You can't be a barber over the internet, and you can't be a bike mechanic over the internet. You have to do it with your hands. It is something that can never be replaced." The 718 Cyclery invites customers to play an integral role in the building process of a bike. They help them choose all the components and the consumer can even help with the bike build. 718 Cyclery calls this service a Therapy Session. The video never discusses the product, because in the eyes of a consumer, the product is not what they're paying for. They are paying for the service and the experience.

Nocella is correct, a bike technician is one role that can never be done online. While a community of riders may be able to buy everything they need from a website, they will have to come through the doors of the IBR for a repair or an adjustment.

Service departments have the potential to grow the business of bike retail in ways we've never thought of. Which is why it is time to stop treating them like an alien experiment. In this chapter we will take a deep dive into the back of the house operations. We will dissect the service department, present some viewpoints you may not have considered, and open up the world of service to help future proof bike retail.

How Well Are Technicians Paid?

According to Salary.com the median annual salary for a bike technician in the United States is $22,337 (The website refers to bike technicians as bicycle repairers. I know, it's horrible.)[4] Compare the bike technicians' salary to the $24,274 given to someone who repairs shoes, $25,188 for janitors, or $29,962 for a groundskeeper or gardener. While I do not intend to demean those professions I believe a bike technicians' skillset is just as varied, if not more so.

When broken down by US state, California was the leader, followed by New York and New Jersey. Alabama, West Virginia, and Mississippi take the last three spots respectively (sample cities in parenthesis).

1. California: $26,983 (San Francisco)
2. New York: $26,045 (New York)
3. New Jersey: $25,509 (Trenton)
4. Alaska: $25,285 (Anchorage)
5. Hawaii: $24,548 (Honolulu)
6. Delaware: $24,436 (Wilmington)
7. Massachusetts: $24,392 (Boston)
8. Washington: $24,101 (Seattle)
9. Connecticut: $23,856 (Hartford)
10. New Hampshire: $23,565 (Nashua)
11. Illinois: $23,431 (Chicago)
12. Michigan: $23,409 (Ann Arbor)
13. Rhode Island: $23,186 (Providence)
14. Maryland: $23,074 (Baltimore)
15. Pennsylvania: $23,007 (Philadelphia)
16. Oregon: $22,828 (Portland)
17. Maine: $22,806 (Portland)

18. Ohio: $22,694 (Cleveland)
19. Louisiana: $22,627 (New Orleans)
20. Colorado: $22,381 (Boulder)
21. Minnesota: $22,337 (Minneapolis-St. Paul)
22. Virginia: $22,314 (Richmond)
23. Georgia: $22,158 (Atlanta)
24. Arizona: $22,158 (Phoenix)
25. Florida: $21,912 (Miami)
26. Nevada: $21,912 (Las Vegas)
27. Indiana: $21,823 (Indianapolis)
28. Missouri: $21,756 (Kansas City)
29. Texas: $21,644 (Austin)
30. Idaho: $21,622 (Boise)
31. Kansas: $21,510 (Wichita)
32. Vermont: $21,399 (Burlington)
33. Utah: $21,332 (Salt Lake City)
34. Kentucky: $21,265 (Lexington)
35. Iowa: $21,198 (Des Moines)
36. Oklahoma: $21,153 (Tulsa)
37. Nebraska: $20,907 (Omaha)
38. North Carolina: $20,863 (Fayetteville)
39. New Mexico: $20,684 (Albuquerque)
40. Wisconsin: $20,550 (Madison)
41. South Carolina: $20,527 (Columbia)
42. North Dakota: $20,103 (Bismarck)
43. South Dakota: $20,014 (Rapid City)
44. Tennessee: $19,924 (Chattanooga)
45. Arkansas: $19,880 (Little Rock)
46. Montana: $19,768 (Billings)
47. Wyoming: $19,701 (Casper)
48. Alabama: $19,634 (Montgomery)
49. West Virginia: $19,433 (Charleston)
50. Mississippi: $18,450 (Jackson)

The NBDA has also run surveys on technician salaries and while comparing surveys is comparing apples to oranges, there is no data from NBDA that could refute the data from Salary.com. The NBDA split their survey between junior and senior mechanics.

From nearly 200 retailers surveyed, the majority of junior mechanics (45.7%) are earning less $15,000 annually while the majority of senior mechanics (39.7%) are earning between $20,000 and $29,999.[5]

Looking at these numbers it's not difficult to see why a bike technician is often someone who loves their work more than money in their pocket. A technician from Colorado confirmed this for me once when he said, "I do this to make a living, not make a killing." Indeed, working in the service department may never equal a six-figure salary as a national median but as an industry we are adept at under-earning and, as a result, underpaying.

When we put aside our inner-monk and the idea that a happy cyclist is all the pay we will ever need, we will encounter the logic of our economy and consumerism. When we accept a lower salary we will inadvertently justify charging less for the services we do. Ultimately we are devaluing much more than ourselves, we are devaluing the products we sell and our industry as a whole.

Working to Code

Tom Sachs is an artist based in New York City. In December of 2012 he posted onto YouTube a guide covering the procedures, work ethic, and work behavior he expects of his studio employees. The video is titled "10 Bullets" and it is a twisted homage to corporate training films by exploring Sachs's exacting studio processes and procedures.[6] To quote Sachs, "This movie series attempts to familiarize employees with both the fundamentals and nuances of the code. Follow this guide carefully and you probably won't be fired."

While the video does come from an entirely different industry, the Ten Bullets relate very well to the day-to-day functions of a service area. I recommend watching the video first (tenbullets.com), and then read my suggestions on how the Ten Bullets can work as an actionable guide for bike technicians.

1. Work To Code - Creativity is the Enemy. When Sachs says "work to code" he is telling us to adhere to the procedures and processes that the studio has put in place. Those processes do not exist to constrain anyone, they exist to simplify all the tasks that should be simplified.

In comparison to all machines, a bike is a very simple one. It is a combination of levers, pulleys, and bearings all operated by a chain drive system. When someone works on a bike they work to a prescribed order. They measure saddle height before putting the bike in the repair stand, set barrel adjusters before adjusting the derailleur, and true the wheels before adjusting the brake calipers. Great technicians understand that to get the bike to function properly the repair work must be done systematically.

Saying 'creativity is the enemy' does not mean to avoid creativity, it suggests that for much of the work creativity and problem solving skills simply are not needed. If a bike technician has a desire to think creatively when he should be thinking systematically it can backfire and cause havoc.

2. Sacred space. A technician's workbench is a sacred space and respect of the space is essential. The film suggests thinking of this space as a shaker workshop or monastery (i.e. no eating burritos on the workbench). When in the sacred space all respect is given to the person doing a task. Unnecessary noises or acts only disrupt the work that needs to be done.

When I discuss the sacred space retailers often ask me if customers should be allowed in the service area. Since it is sacred space there is a fear that customers will cause distractions. There is also a question on whether or not a technician should hide the magic, keep a layer of mystery over how the work is done so customers will always need us.

Here is my view, a service area is like the kitchen at a house party; everybody wants to be in the kitchen. IBRs that have open service areas for their customers have a greater sense of community. The goal is to create a kitchen-like feel while giving technicians the space, time, and focus they need to effectively do the job. A large retailer can achieve this by having two service areas, one for customers to do bike check-ins and on-the-fly repairs, the other for work that needs more focus. A smaller retailer could consider building a bar that gives the customers a place to engage but creates a barrier from the technicians.

3. Be on time. There is an obvious explanation for this rule. Be on time can mean just that, be on time. If the shift starts at 9:00am, be ready to work at 9:00am. Though I prefer to schedule people 15-30 minutes prior to their shift starting.

The less obvious explanation is that when we ask people to be on time we are asking them to commit themselves entirely to their work and to have an on the clock mentality. Timmy can be at his workbench at 9:00am like he was asked but that doesn't mean Timmy is ready to work. Timmy should take care of himself, eat and drink in a manner that will allow him to do his best work. Staying out all night, getting drunk and stumbling in at 9:00am is disrespectful to management, his coworkers, and himself. Timmy's present tasks demand his fullest attention.

4. Be thorough. Many technicians will remember a time where they've spent several hours doing a complete overhaul on a bike only to realize they've forgot to tighten the stem when the customer grabs the bike and the handlebar flies sideways. The little things can sometimes make the biggest impact. If the customer paid $150 for repair work and the technician forgot to tighten the stem the question running through their mind is, "What else did he forget to do?" When technicians take the time to be thorough it shows customers respect and appreciation for their patronage.

Being thorough shows coworkers respect as well. A thorough technician will notice when the shop is almost out of brake housing and will make sure to get more in stock. A thorough technician will not just complete a task but also be constantly preparing for the next tasks.

5. Give feedback, get feedback. In a service area one person must make sure the other person receives the information sent. In the 10 Bullets video they use the phrase "I understand". By saying 'I understand' technicians are ensuring that they are on the same page as the person they're working with.

Giving and receiving feedback is a two way street. It is important to give information in a manner that does not create more questions. If the manager asks Timmy to build a Stumpjumper to stock on the floor, this is poor communication. Which model of Stumpjumper? Which size? Which color? In this case poor communication from the manager could spark more questions, or worse, Timmy could spend the next hour building a bike that there is no need for. Managers should be sure to communicate in a clear manner that answers any obvious follow-up questions. Such communication might sound like this, "Timmy, could you please build a Stumpjumper Comp HT, in white, size large, and have it priced and ready to ride before two o'clock today?"

6. Sent does not mean received. This is a great rule to use when working with customers. When checking in a bike a technician should consider having the customer sign and agree to the quote (side note: quotes should always have a 10-20% buffer for additional purchases that may not have been seen in the initial estimate). When a bike is finished the technician should contact the customer by phone, if they do not answer then send an email, if they still do not answer consider sending a text. In each instance asking them to respond to confirm they've received the message.

7. Keep a list. A list is more than a series of tasks to accomplish. A list is a record of what has been done and still needs to be done. Keeping a list is so important in bike retail that I have dedicated an entire section to checklists.

8. Always be knolling (ABK). According to Wikipedia, "Knolling is the process of arranging like objects in parallel or 90 degree angles as a method of organization."[7] Here is how Sachs teaches knolling:

- Scan your environment for materials, tools, books, music, etc. which are not in use.

- Put away everything not in use. If you aren't sure, leave it out.

- Group all like objects

- Align or square all objects to either the surface they rest on, or the studio itself.

A perfectly knolled work bench keeps life simple, clean, and professional. Using the ABK rule in the service area means every time a tool or part is set it down on the workbench it is set at 90 degrees to the table. Over time, the greater organization will result in greater efficiency and faster work.

9. Sacrifice to Leatherface. Leatherface was the inbred, chainsaw-carrying psychopath from the movie Texas Chainsaw Massacre. In 10 Bullets a Leatherface doll sits on top of a deposit box. If someone breaks a rule, they pay a fine, hence the title, Sacrifice to Leatherface.

This is an important rule to have in the store. If there are no consequences for mistakes, laziness, or forgetfulness then there is no external motivation to perform work well. In the video Sachs chooses money as the sacrifice to Leatherface. Slamming the door, showing up late, or not having a pen and paper handy to make a list means paying a monetary fine. The fines are not meant as punishment, but rather as a lesson in taking responsibility for actions and establishing a process-oriented behavior in the studio. An example of fostering this behavior is illustrated well when Sachs tells his staff that leaving the lights on is a $5.00 fine, but the fine doubles for each instance. So leaving the lights on eleven times will cost $5120.00. My guess is that Sachs' staff never leaves the lights on more than two or three times.

Monetary fines may not be the cultural norm for many retailers. So here are some examples of how to create sacrifices to Leatherface in an IBR.

- Every time you drop a tool you do five push-ups.

- If you do not tell someone or place an order for an out of stock item you clean everyone's benches at the end of the day.

- If you forget to add an item to a ticket you clean the employee bathroom every day for a week.

- When you are late for work someone else chooses which bikes you work on.

I would avoid sacrifices that results in a positive. Having someone buy beer when they make mistakes may encourage the mistake more than prevent it.

10. Persistence. "Press on. Nothing in the world can take the place of persistence. Talent will not; nothing is more common than unsuccessful men with talent. Genius will not; the world is full of educated derelicts. Persistence and determination alone are omnipotent"

Sachs' tenth bullet was a direct quote from Ray Kroc, the founder of McDonalds,[8] and it illustrates the value of persistence beautifully. While Kroc's quote could have been talking about the persistence of pushing through repetitive work I prefer to think he was speaking of something more profound. In bike retail many people can get caught up in the minutiae of day to day tasks. Many managers and technicians often leave bigger and more important goals on the backburner while saying that they'll, "get to it tomorrow". Don't forget it and don't push it off any more than it needs to; be persistent.

Breaking Down the Tune-Up

Tune-ups come by many names: performance tune-up, complete tune-up, pro tune-up, standard tune-up, bronze, silver, and gold tune-ups. I've seen tune-ups named after triathlons: sprint tune-up, Olympic tune-up, and Ironman tune-up. I've seen tune-ups named after racer categories: cat 3 tune-up, cat 2 tune-up, and cat 1 tune-up. I've even seen tune-ups named after the type of bike: road tune-up, mountain tune-up, and hybrid tune-up.

No matter what the tune-up has been named the work that is being done is generally the same, regardless of which IBR is performing the service. Having been in over 500 bike retailers I have found that there is nothing more common and generalized than the tune-up. For every store I've visited the list of services offered during a tune-up are practically identical from store to store. They are:

Adjust braking and shifting.
Spot true the wheels.
Lube the chain.
Clean the bike.
Inflate the tires.
Set the suspension.
Check torque on all the bolts.

There might be slight differences from one IBR to another, but this is the meat of what everyone is selling. Imagine how confusing this can be for a customer, especially when one IBR names their services something completely different than the other retailers in town. Add to that the prices are different, the turns around times are different, the repair stations look different, and on the surface they're performing an identical service. This leaves many customers baffled, struggling to determine what is the true difference between different retailers. Here are the steps I would recommend to make tune-up services stand out.

Stop using the word "tune". Everyone uses it and it sparks a lot of confusion. I would also stay away from the terms "basic" or "checkup". These words imply a service that does not require much expertise or involve a lot of work. Instead, I would refer to them as services. Yes, everyone uses the word services but it is used at a higher level to describe everything done, not just this specific work.

Start speaking in the customers' language. In an IBR words like caliper, derailleur, press fit, BB30, 3-cross, guide pulley, tension pulley, 31.8, 27.2, 27.5, 700c, and 172.5 are common language. For a lot of customers these words might as well be Finnish. Customers don't understand when a technician tells them she is adjusting the calipers, but they will understand her when she says she'll be providing perfect braking.

Focus on differentiators. If a technician measures saddle height before and after every service to ensure the bike is returned as they received it, this is a service that can be featured. It is a small thing and it may be something that has been done for years, but it is the small features that may resonate with customers. Some other features many IBRs already offer but could be promoting more:

Using nontoxic cleaners
Using lint free rags
24-hour turn around
Delivery
Weighing the bike
Follow up phone call
Full inventory of replacement parts
Safety storage (bike won't touch other bikes)
All settings set to rider weight or ride preferences
Guarantee on service
Text notification when finished

Name services something that will never be copied. The best example I have seen of this was from a bike shop where the owner named his services the 1988, 1991, and 1992. These services signified the years he had won the state road cycling championship. No one will ever take those names from him and they spark a great story every time.

Increase professionalism. Cleaning the workbench after each repair, wearing a uniform, and speaking with empathy all increase professionalism. Don't underestimate the value of an apron either. A clean apron in a service area is like a white coat in the hospital. It symbolizes the most knowledgeable person in the room. I encourage all technicians to wear them with pride.

Is the Future Bright for Bike Technicians?

A report by Bloomberg Businessweek showing their calculations of US Bureau of Labor Statistics, which was reported on BikeBiz.com, stated "The fastest-growing professions in the US include home-health aide, translator and event planner. But, perhaps not surprisingly given the current strength of the 'bikeconomy', the profession of bike mechanic is also on the list of fastest growing jobs in the US"[9]

Is the future really bright for bike technicians? From my view, yes the future is extremely bright but a bright future for a technician does not guarantee a bright future for the IBR they work in. We must separate the two.

First, retailers who have seen growth in the past decade have done so in a relatively flat "bikeconomy". The number of bikes sold in the US has not drastically changed in the last fifteen years. Meaning the pie is not getting bigger, but for some retailers their slice of the pie is. This leads to fewer bike shops selling a lot more. For example, we can look at retailers like Mike's Bikes in Northern California with over 10 locations, Erik's Bike & Board in the Midwest with over 20 locations, or Bike Source across the central US. Each business has grown and opened new locations in the past decade. Will these retailers reach a place where they stop growing? Looking at their history and how they've managed to expand, it's doubtful. As these businesses grow, if they are not creating new cyclists to match their rate of their growth, then their growth is through obtaining market share. The result, smaller bike retailers will get pushed out by larger ones. How does this tectonic shift in the industry affect a bike technician? It means the number of technicians may not change- they will just have fewer places to work.

Second, looking at a spark line over the past decade, margins for IBDs have continued to drop while taxes and fixed costs continue to rise. This shrinking margin will force retailers to focus on high margin services like repair, fitting, coaching, consultation, and possibly event management. Once these services are treated as a strong revenue center rather than necessary evils of the business, the industry will be in dire need of extremely professional and skilled technicians.

For bike technicians today, I recommend three areas of focus to ensure a career that is in high demand and high pay going forward.

Incredible customer service. On par with any business that leads in customer service. Technicians might have solution sales skills now, but will need insight selling skills in the future. The ability to paint a clear picture of what is to come in every customer's future and offering the products and services to properly experience it.

Electronics. We can expect more ebikes, electronic shifting, navigation systems, and integration with apps. It will not be long before a bicycle has many of the same features as a car. Rebuilding, rebooting and rewiring an ebike is a completely different skill set than currently exists in most service areas. Imagine when electronic systems exist on all bikes and the technician's job consists of hooking up the bike to a diagnostics machine and updating software applications.

Social communication. Communicating with customers through social channels will only grow and the technician will always be the voice of expertise in the store. Tweeting services and how-to tips to customers will happen with greater frequency and the technicians that lead the way will win the largest amount of their local market. Earning a great amount of respect in the process.

I agree with the Bloomberg calculations.[10] The future is bright for bike technicians, but only the ones whose skillsets grow at the same rate as the technologies they are working on.

Engineering a Service Menu

In the service area, the service menu is the single most important document an owner, manager, or technician can write. The service menu is, in many ways, the business plan, marketing statement, P&L, and training menu. When a menu is built well a technician shouldn't have to sell what is on the menu, the menu should sell itself. Building and designing a service menu is called menu engineering, a combination of psychology, managerial accounting, marketing, and graphic design. The restaurant industry dedicates millions to menu engineering every year. Restaurants understand that a properly engineered menu can garner up to a 20% increase in sales which is why they do not take menus it lightly.

During the financial crisis in 2009 restaurants were hit very hard. People just didn't want to spend the money to go out and eat. While some restaurateurs were scrambling to get more people in the doors others were focused on getting more money from the customers they had, and they did this by taking a closer look at their menus. In December of 2009 the New York Times published an article on how menu engineering was coming to the forefront for many restaurants. "Pounded by the recession, they are hoping that some magic combination of prices, adjectives, fonts, types sizes, ink colors and placement on the page can coax diners into spending a little more money."[11]

Every item on the service menu can be broken up into four specific offerings. Those categories are:

Stars. Stars are extremely popular and have a high profit margin. Ideally Stars should be the flagship or signature menu items. Fixing a flat tire and a tune-up are Stars in most service areas.

Workhorses. Workhorses are high in popularity but low in profit margin. This is usually because the money earned from a workhorse is lower than the standard hourly rate. Workhorse menu items sell well, but don't significantly increase revenue.

Puzzles. Puzzles are difficult to sell yet high in profit margin. For many service areas the 50-hour suspension service falls into this category.

Dogs. Dogs are difficult to sell and low in profit margin.

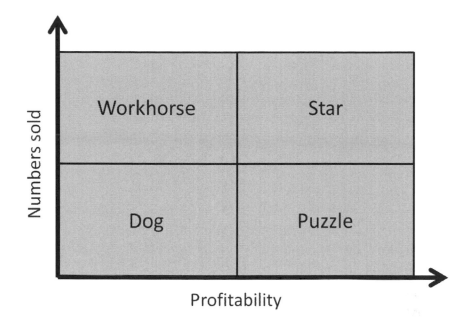

Fig 5.2: All services offered will fall into one of these four categories

Once a retailer has categorized their services the goal is to guide customers to purchasing the stars, and the one service bike retailers likely sell the most of is their tune-up. This is because the tune-up is a universal service. Every customer with a bike needs a tune-up at some time, ideally once or twice every year. The tune-up is the service that can backlog technicians for weeks in peak season. The tune-up is by every definition, a star menu item.

The Science of Service Menus

A question I challenge many IBRs to answer is how to get their star services to produce as much revenue as possible while at the same time giving customers more options to buy and a customized service.

The most successful answer I've seen executed is to offer four tune-up services instead of one. A menu of one means the customer has no choices. The customer has no way to buy more and the technician has no clear way to upsell the package. Having four tune-up services will appeal to the price conscious shopper, the lost shopper, and the price-is-no-object shopper. Here is an example of a four tier tune-up menu.

Tune-up Menu:
Level 1 Service: $230
Level 2 Service: $100
Level 3 Service: $70
Level 4 Service: $30

First I will explain the psychology of the pricing structure and then I will present ideas for what can be included in each service.

Retailers who are using this pricing structure have shown the most popular selling items on the menu will be Level 2 and Level 3. With the scale tipping just slightly toward the Level 3 Service. Level 1 takes roughly 10% of the orders and Level 4 takes only 5%. When compared to an $80 tune-up, we can break down the potential growth:

$80 x 100 sales = $8000

or

$230 x 10 sales = $2300
$100 x 40 sales = $4000
$70 x 45 sales = $3150
$30 x 5 sales = $150

The second scenario brings in $9600; a 20% growth. So why does this work?

First, Level 4 ($30) service will always be the worst seller. No one wants to purchase the worst option of anything. Level 4 Service is focused on the truly price conscious.

Level 1 ($230) will cater to those customers who have purchased high ticket items. If someone buys a $9000 bike they deserve the option to buy a more comparable service than someone who buys a $900 bike.

Level 2 and 3 ($100 and $70 respectively) are for customers who are not sure what they want. Notice the gap between these levels is the smallest price gap on the menu. The jump from Level 3 to Level 2 was $10 cheaper than the jump from Level 1 to Level 2. Since the majority of people buy in the middle, we want the middle to have options.

Below is a formula for creating a service menu using these pricing tactics. Start by taking the price of the most popular tune-up, that will be X. From there multiply out each level and round out to the nearest 5 or 0.

Level 1: 3.25X
Level 2: 1.5X
Level 3: X
Level 4: 0.45X

Once the pricing structure is set, the next step is to define what is offered in each service. Here is my recommendation.

Level 4 ($30)
Bike inspection
Bolt/torque check
Lube drivetrain
Inflate tires

In many ways Level 4 Service acts as a quote or estimate. The bike inspection is where the value of this purchase is. Many people who purchase this package will often walk away with an idea of what services need to be done the next time they return.

Level 3 ($70)
Everything in Level 4
Perfect braking
Perfect shifting
Wheel inspection and adjustment

The Level 3 Service is, as many bike retailers would define it, the standard tune-up. Notice that I stayed away from using technical terminology. Telling someone to purchase a "wheel true" can be confusing so I opted for "wheel inspection and adjustment".

Level 2 ($100)
Everything in Level 3
Remove chain and cassette, clean with solvent
Complete wash, lust, and detailing

Since most people will be choosing between Level 2 and 3, the best carrot is kept in Level 2. Cleaning parts with solvent and offering a wash, lust, and detailing is a huge hook for people to make the jump. Many technicians have spent hours trying to get something to shift properly and when the customer saw the bike they were only excited by how clean it looked. A clean bike is something the customer can see, it makes sense to them. A perfect shifting bike is expected and can't be enjoyed until after they leave the bike shop.

Level 1 ($230)
Everything in Level 2
New brake pads
New cables
New bar tape or grips
Remove brakes, crankset, and derailleurs- clean with solvent

In order to justify higher prices in the service area begin tying parts to the costs of service. New brake pads, cables, and bar tape or grips are key elements to making the bike work as if it were new off the floor. Someone buying in at this level expects a perfect machine in every way, and these are just the services that will achieve it. It is worth noting that the Level 1 buyer is also the buyer who is most susceptible to additional sales like a new saddle, new tires, or even a new wheelset. If a technician sees the opportunity, they should never be afraid to ask.

The Art of Service Menus

Once the science of the service menu has been determined it comes time to add the art, which means design. Great design tells a story. It doesn't have to have a beginning, middle and end, but some kind of narrative must exist, some sense of time and place— context is everything when it comes to menu design. Here are some steps to follow when designing the perfect service menu.

Reinforce the store's brand image. If the store is sleek and clean, the menu should be as well. If the store has a laidback mom-and-pop vibe, then the menu should reflect that as well. Visit http://www.underconsideration.com/artofthemenu/ to view hundreds of menus from restaurants all around the world. These menus can be used as a reference point when hiring a graphic designer.

I cannot stress enough the value of hiring a designer. Unless someone working at the retailer has been employed as a graphic designer in the past, I would discourage doing the design in-house. It will be worth the few hundred bucks to have it done right. For retailers that don't know any designers I suggest using www.99designs.com, on this site retailers will be able to post their design needs and have designers bid for the contract.

Build the menu as people would read it. People read a menu the same way they read a book- sequentially, moving their eyes from left to right and down the page or pages. For a service menu I would plan on people taking their time to read it. Bike services can be complicated and confusing, so customers will take a moment to understand what has been written.

Drop the dollar sign. According to a study by The Center for Hospitality Research at Cornell University,[12] on average, customers spent 8% more when prices were in numerals with no dollar sign (50) versus in dollars and cents ($50) or written out (fifty dollars). While we're at it, lose the 99. The 1920s are over, a penny means nothing, and everyone is aware of this lame attempt at psychological trickery. End prices with a number that ends in 0 or 5.

Keep it legible. That means choosing a font size that is large enough and has enough contrast to stand out against the background. I would avoid cursive and using all-capital letters except for the very shortest runs of letters, such as SERVICES. A quick Google image search for "bike shop service menus" will produce a series of menus that could be mistaken for pages in a textbook. In a service menu, a lot of reading is a bad thing.

Use graphics to give items a shout out. Shaded boxes, outlined boxes, type and color changes, photos, and other graphic treatments draw the eye to the star services. Trust the designer on this one, tell them what services the store sells the most and where growth is needed. Designers will be able to build the menu to be as effective as possible.

Be descriptive but not too descriptive. Strive for copy that explains the service without going overboard. There is a happy medium between too little copy (flat fix) and describing every detail on which tools are used and the value of talcing a tube. Remember to steer clear of language that is too confusing. "Perfect braking" is better than "adjusting brake calipers".

Check the spelling. And then check it again. And again. Then give it to trusted friends and customers to review it. I have posted my menu on social media before and asked for feedback. It's free and a great way to test how customers will respond.

Print little and print big. Most service areas will want two menus, one that is handed to the customer and one that hangs in the service area for everyone to read. The one that hangs in the service area should not be a duplicate of the printed version. The large hanging piece should focus on the top 4-6 services, no more. Details should be reserved for the printed piece. Hang the sign so it is viewable by customers when they are checking in the bike, for some retailers this may mean it hangs in the back of the service area.

Keep it clean. Too many service menus are grease stained pieces of paper stuffed away in a 3-ring binder. With so many options for desktop publishing, have menus printed out and encourage the customer to take it with them. On the store's website offer the menu in a PDF format so customers can view it the way it was intended to be viewed.

By increasing the services offered IBRs provide choice to their customers, they are competitive in the market by being the cheapest and most expensive at the same time, and they add directly to the bottom line. By designing the menu effectively the retailer puts everything into context and everyone's job gets easier. It's easier for customers to choose what they'd like to purchase and it's easier for everyone in the store to sell the service.

Checking In Bikes

The most critical moment in any bike repair is the check-in and performing a proper check-in requires a very specific skillset. Ideally the person who does a bike check-in is one of the most knowledgeable and mechanically inclined people in the store, they are personable and adept at reading the customer, they have no problem making suggestions for upgrades and they do it a way that adds value to the rider- not in a way that sounds like they're just trying to milk more money from them. When this person isn't doing the check-in and Timmy is on the front lines many things can go wrong.

If a bike check-in is not done properly then it can send a ripple of inefficiency through the entire service area. If Timmy misses a frayed cable or a cracked seatpost this can put the repair on hold while the technician has to contact the customer, apologize, and explain why the bill is going to be higher than quoted. Everyone looks inept in this scenario.

There are four ways to help Timmy do better when he has to perform the bike check-in. First, have a great menu using all the strategies we've previously discussed. Second, quote all services with a 15-20% buffer. This buffer will allow the technician to spend a little money should they encounter something that needs replaced. Third is to use a thorough checklist when doing the check-in. This is a checklist will carefully walk through a bike starting at the front and moving to the back.

When technicians perform a check-in working from the front of the bike to the back it creates a consistent system that will leave minimal guesswork and reduce the risk of missing something. Here is a checklist to get started:

F. Tire: tread wear, cracking
F. Rim: trueness, pad burn, cracking, swelling
F. Spokes: loose or snapped
F. Hub: lateral play, stickiness, QR loose
F. Rotor: wear, warped
F. Caliper: pad wear, cable fray
Fork: compression/rebound not responsive
HT: cracks at TT and DT junction
Headset: fore/aft play with fork
Stem: not straight, bolts loose/uneven
Handlebar: not center, odd rotation
Computer: Not working
F. Light: Not working
Bar tape/grips: wear
Shifters/brake levers: squishy, loose, difficult to move
DT: bottle cage loose, broken
BB: cracks at DT, CS, and ST junction
Crankset: lateral play, loose bolts
Chainring: loose/missing bolts, worn teeth
Chain: stretch, how many miles?
Pedals: sticky, rusted, bolts stripped
F. Derailleur: Not shifting properly, cable fray
ST: bottle cage loose, linkage sticky, cracks at TT/SS junction
Seatpost: over max height, scratched, not dropping
Saddle: sagging, rails loose, material wear
SS: Shock compression/rebound not responsive
R. Light: Not working
R. Caliper: pad wear, cable fray
R. Rotor: wear, warped
R. Hub: lateral play, stickiness, QR loose
R. Spokes: loose or snapped
R. Cassette: play, worn teeth
R. Derailleur: Not shifting properly, worn pulleys, cable fray

R. Rim: trueness, pad burn, cracking, swelling

R. Tire: tread wear, cracking

I would encourage technicians to put a check next to every box once it has been inspected. If the technician finds a problem the customer should be aware of, he adds notes to the checklist. Of course thoroughness and legibility are always important; if possible it is best to have this checklist done on a computer.

The fourth and final way to win at the bike check-in is to ask great questions about how the bike has been used and what inspired the customer to bring it in. Here are the questions I would ask.

Name?

Phone?

Email?

Best way to contact? Phone? Email? Text? Tweet?

Address?

When do you need the bike back?

Which of the menu items would you feel suits you best?

Any odd sounds? Clinks? Clanks? Rubbing?

Anything feel weird or uncomfortable?

Any pain in your body when riding?

Where have you ridden it since your last service?

How many miles since your last service (estimate)?

Do you have an event coming up?

What is most important to you: speed or comfort?

Using this structure will take the technician to the next level when performing a check-in. It won't be fun to switch to this new checklist, but when it is done the customer experience is improved, work efficiency and profit will all increase while costs decrease.

What Would You Say
You Do Here?

Many IBRs tell me that they have the best service department. They would confidently stack up their team against any other team of technicians in the world. When they tell me this, I can absolutely see their pride shine through, they are truly proud of the services they offer. However, I like to remind them that no one has ever told me something to the contrary. No one has said, "Our service department is full of lazy idiots who hate customers and crotch floss with every bike they get." If everyone's service is the best, how does the customer tell anyone apart?

Below I have pulled three service descriptions from bike shops in the US. I have changed nothing except the name of the store.

BIKE SHOP A: Our service staff is ready to work on all makes and models of bicycles, not just the ones we sell. Whether it's a minor tune-up or a major overhaul, you can count on us to do the job right the first time. When you bring in your bike for service, we always start with a free, no-obligation estimate of the work that will be needed. One of our service pros will discuss the problem with you and will carefully explain what work should be done, always respecting your choices and your budget.

BIKE SHOP B: BIKE SHOP B's bicycle service department will provide you an unparalleled experience regardless of what ails your bike. From flat tire repairs to complete suspension overhauls, our service professionals will evaluate your bike and determine exactly what services you require. Our bicycle maintenance team has years of experience and special training to deal with any issue that you may have. We take pride in our professional, prompt service and strive to offer you the best possible bicycle maintenance available.

BIKE SHOP C: BIKE SHOP C is committed to keeping your bike working perfectly. Whether you need a small adjustment, a maintenance visit or a major overhaul, our experienced mechanics ensure your service is prompt and complete. No wonder so many people choose our service department for regular maintenance and unexpected repairs. Because we stock a wealth of upgrades and replacement components – even hard-to-find sizes – we can get your bike back to you right away, with parts that fit precisely. Since we're every-day riders, too, we can also offer good advice, money-saving tips and practical solutions to whatever challenge you meet on a Main street. A well-maintained, well-adjusted bicycle is a joy to ride, so smart riders know the value of excellent service. They bring their bikes to BIKE SHOP C

If any of these bike shops made someone feel more special than another I would be surprised. They have all achieved at saying, more or less, the exact same thing. Everyone has experienced and trained staff, everyone can provide a full range of services, and everyone can work on all makes and models. When we write these type of statements we can often fall into the trap of trying to be all things to all people.

From these three service descriptions I've gone the next logical step and created a formula for designing a bland service center description.

At [BIKE SHOP NAME] our [ADJECTIVE] staff is committed to providing the best [THING YOU'RE SELLING]. From a [EASY THING] to a [DIFFICULT THING] our [ADJECTIVE] staff with over [NUMBER] years of experience will [VERB] you to the [THING CUSTOMER WANTS]. At [BIKE SHOP NAME] you will receive the best [ANOTHER THING CUSTOMER WANTS]. We have a [ADJECTIVE] selection of parts from [BRAND 1] and [BRAND 2] but will service all makes and models. We have [NUMBER] hour service, and a [ADJECTIVE] shopping experience. We look forward to seeing you soon.

Please do not use this template, it is a joke. Instead follow the advice of author William Arruda. In his book Ditch Dare Do, Arruda teaches people to "work your quirks" or in other words, focus what makes the business or services unique because that is what will truly stand out in a crowded market.[13]

121

I encourage all retailers to define their services in a new and exciting way and describe what makes them the best or most unique. Start by answering these questions:

What do you do that no one else does?
What do your customers call you?
What bikes do you love working on?

Trying to be everything to everyone makes the business sound bland and corporate. Instead, I ask IBRs to focus on one person, they're ideal customer, and write as if they were only talking to him or her.

Chapter 5
Vansevenant Checklist

Watch "Ten Bullets" by Tom Sachs: http://bit.ly/1b9w7Dx

With your service staff, define how the Ten Bullets can work in your bike shop.

1. Work to code
2. Sacred space
3. Be on time
4. Be thorough
5. Give feedback, get feedback
6. Sent does not mean received
7. Keep a list
8. Always be knolling
9. Sacrifice to Leatherface
10. Persistence

Engineer the perfect service menu by defining your stars, workhorses, puzzles, and dogs.

Create a tune-up menu offering four service options using this formula:

Level 1: 3.25X
Level 2: 1.5X
Level 3: X (current price for a tune-up)
Level 4: 0.45X

Choose some menus you like from: http://bit.ly/19dp7RW

Hire a designer to redesign the service menu. If you can't find a designer consider using http://99designs.com

Build a checklist for checking in bikes. Use this as starting point:

Things to ask the customer:
Name?
Phone?
Email?
Best way to contact? Phone? Email? Text? Tweet?
Address?
When do you need the bike back?
Which of our menu items would you feel suits you best?
Any odd sounds? Clinks? Clanks? Rubbing?
Anything feel weird or uncomfortable?
Any pain in your body when riding?
Where have you ridden it since your last service?
How many miles since your last service (estimate)?
Do you have an event coming up?
What is most important to you: speed or comfort?

Items to check on the bike:
F. Tire: tread wear, cracking
F. Rim: trueness, pad burn, cracking, swelling
F. Spokes: loose or snapped
F. Hub: lateral play, stickiness, QR loose
F. Rotor: wear, warped
F. Caliper: pad wear, cable fray

Fork: compression/rebound not responsive
HT: cracks at TT and DT junction
Headset: fore/aft play with fork
Stem: not straight, bolts loose/uneven
Handlebar: not center, odd rotation
Computer: Not working
F. Light: Not working
Bar tape/grips: wear
Shifters/brake levers: squishy, loose, difficult to move
DT: bottle cage loose, broken
BB: cracks at DT, CS, and ST junction
Crankset: lateral play, loose bolts
Chainring: loose/missing bolts, worn teeth
Chain: stretch, how many miles?
Pedals: sticky, rusted, bolts stripped
F. Derailleur: Not shifting properly, cable fray
ST: bottle cage loose, linkage sticky, cracks at TT/SS junction
Seatpost: over max height, scratched, not dropping
Saddle: sagging, rails loose, material wear
SS: Shock compression/rebound not responsive
R. Light: Not working
R. Caliper: pad wear, cable fray
R. Rotor: wear, warped
R. Hub: lateral play, stickiness, QR loose
R. Spokes: loose or snapped
R. Cassette: play, worn teeth
R. Derailleur: Not shifting properly, worn pulleys, cable fray
R. Rim: trueness, pad burn, cracking, swelling
R. Tire: tread wear, cracking

Rewrite the service description on the website. Focus on one person, you're ideal customer, and write as if you were only talking to him or her. Make it special and make it unique.

What do you do that no one else does?
What do your customers call you?
What bikes do you love working on?

6

Managing Leadouts

"I think every cyclist should look a little outside, open up their horizons a little bit and listen and look into other things that are fun. Do what you like and profit from that."
- Jens Voigt, professional cyclist

Why do people buy bicycles? The most common answers are fitness, fun, competition, and adventure. But these are the same answers for buying a set of running shoes, a tennis racket, or a swimsuit. All being more affordable and holding a lower barrier to entry as well. By answering the question "why people buy a bike?" retailers can understand their customers better and guide them to a life as a cyclist. I have listed out 16 specific reasons why people will buy a bike.

The bike they are buying meets their basic needs. They absolutely need a bike to function in their life. Perhaps a bicycle is their only means of transportation or a tool they use for work. As a former bike messenger I've purchased many bikes to meet nothing more than a basic need but this is not the most popular reason for purchasing a bike in North America. Bikes are not a base need for most people, they are a luxury item.

Convenience. Some buy because the purchase has been made easy. Maybe the retailer is the closest one for miles. Maybe the retailer is the only one who carries the product they are looking for. Or perhaps, in some way, the customer has been convinced that cycling is the easiest sport to do. Convenience can be a big motivator to purchase. This is why Starbucks is fine opening two locations across the street from each other.

Replacement. Sometimes people buy a bike because they need to replace their old bike. This replacement could be for logical reasons (their old bike was stolen), for performance reasons (the newer bike is 70 grams lighter), or for egotistical reasons (they want the newest thing before their friend gets it).

Scarcity. Perhaps the bike is a collectible or limited edition. When scarcity is a motivation to purchase a bike some may hope to gain return on the investment, buying a bike ridden by a Tour de France champion for example. I've seen some IBRs that are brilliant at turning old or used stock into a scarce collectible-though they have to hold on to the bikes much longer than most are comfortable with.

Prestige or ego. A bike that is purchased to boost one's esteem. Perhaps he or she wants to impress their friends and be the first one with this bike. Perhaps they are looking for people to notice them.

As a tool for change. Many people buy a bike to get healthier or for rehabilitation after an injury. While many retailers are brilliant at selling bikes not many are good at keeping people on the bike. Often times, within 6 months, the bike that was purchased as a tool of change finds its way to the garage rafters.

Emotional vacuum. Sometimes people buy a bike in place of buying something they could never have. Someone may never own a McLaren car, but they could own a Specialized McLaren.

Low price. If a person is not considering a bike purchase, a price will never convince them to buy a bike. Any bike that has ever been sold was sold to someone who made the decision to buy long before they saw the price. A low or reasonable price provides the logical justification to buy, not the motivation.

Great value. Sometimes the value of a bike greatly exceeds the price. This purchase may not be something needed, it just may be too great of a deal to pass up. This is ideally the underlying tone of any sales event. Sadly though, many retailers tend to focus on low price rather than great value.

Name recognition. Branding can play a big role in someone's willingness to purchase. Just ask any non-Trek retailer who was selling bikes between 1999 and 2005- during Lance Armstrong's seven Tour de France victories (or not-victories, however you see it). In those seven years people were not asking for a road bike, they were asking for a Trek by name.

Fad. In its infancy any new idea can seem like a fad. Clincher tires, full suspension mountain bikes, and aero bars were all touted as fads when they first appeared. People who buy a product because it is new may be following a fad, or they may be early adopters to a new and innovative trend. Only time will tell.

Compulsory purchase. This is when an external force prompts people to buy a bike. They are no longer driving their car or their bike got stolen are two common examples but the most common I have seen is when a child is asking for a bike on their birthday.

Niche identity or peer pressure. This works very well in the case of local cycling clubs and teams. In these niches bike purchase help create a bond within the community. No one wants to be the outcast on a cycling team not riding the team bike.

Gift. Many bike retailers consider the month of December as another buying season. I have seen one bike shop go as far as creating a gift registry for the holidays, weddings, graduations, and any other gift-worthy event.

Empathy. Sometimes people will buy because they care about the store and want to see it succeed, or at least see it sell this particular bike. This reason for buying is nearly dead in bike retail; people have less concern for the retailer's wellbeing.

Addiction. I believe this is vastly under hyped in IBRs, people can get addicted to buying bikes. Some stores have customers that will buy the newest and greatest bike every year. This is addiction, plain and simple.

Fear. Sometimes people do not feel confident with the bike they have. I have seen this happen when someone buys a full suspension mountain bike that will never leave city streets. They fear that the quality of the roads will exceed their skill as a cyclist.

As we go through the list it becomes easy to see that there is a lot happening within ever bike purchase. We're not just selling tubes of aluminum and carbon. People aren't buying just for fun, fitness, or adventure. With so many variables in play the next question I would have is, "How do we build a sales process to address all of these unique buying factors?"

Forty years ago sales experts would have said that in order to be a great salesperson, a person needs to be great at communicating and reading people. They would have said retailers needed to have extensive product knowledge on everything they sold. They would have taught about prospecting, generating leads, managing referrals, and twenty different ways to "close the sale". They would also mention that very few people can become truly great salespeople.

However the 80s, 90s, and 00s have all passed and today is a new day in bike retail. For an IBR planning to be around for the next 10-20 years I would recommend to stop focusing on how to sell a bike but rather focus on how people buy a bike.

While less than 15% of purchases today are happening online, more than 90% of all major purchases start online; usually through research.[1] Most people grab their phone, tablet, or laptop and search a phrase like "best mountain bike". Others may start by posting a tweet, by reading a manufacturers product page, or maybe even reading consumer reviews. Whatever their form of research is, if it was inspiring enough to get them off the couch and walking into the store (which is no small feat, retailers should feel honored when this happens) That is a clear sign that research is nearly over and they are ready to buy. Now it's up to the people working to help the customer or completely screw it up. To help the customer staff do not need even half of the skills mentioned before. To truly help a customer, retailers need to do one simple thing; stop trying to be a salesperson.

Seller Beware

If someone were to ask me to pick the greatest movie ever made which involved salesmen, I would pick 1992's Glengarry Glen Ross.[2] If they went on to ask what made the movie amazing I would surely say, "Blake's speech". The iconic speech by Blake, played by Alec Baldwin, was given to a struggling group of salesmen. Blake makes the trip from downtown, through the rain, and attempts to motivate the team with a sales contest.

He starts his speech by saying, "We're adding a little something to this month's sales contest. As you all know, first prize is a Cadillac Eldorado. Anyone want to see second prize? Second prize is a set of steak knives. Third prize is- you're fired. You get the picture? You're laughing now? You got leads. Mitch and Murray paid good money. Get their names to sell them! You can't close the leads you're given, you can't close shit, you ARE shit, hit the bricks pal and beat it 'cause you are going out!"

In an interview with NPR Daniel Pink, author of To Sell is Human, says that this relentless, predator-style approach to selling has become outdated and that the art of sales has changed more in the past 10 years than it did in the previous century.[3] When asked about the verbally abusive and conniving sales tactics that were illustrated so well in Glengarry Glen Ross, Pink said this, "Most of what we know about sales was built for a world of information asymmetry. The seller always had more information than the buyer. Twenty years ago when you walked into a Chevy dealer, the Chevy dealer knew a heck of a lot more about cars than you ever could ... you didn't have the adequate information. And so this is why we have the principle of caveat emptor, buyer beware. You gotta beware when the other guy knows a lot more than you."

If bike retailers have attended a sales seminar in the past fifty years odds are very good they were taught solution sales techniques. Solution sales teaches retailers how to build an elaborate greeting, offer a company history or building tour, ask a laborious list of questions, identify a customer need or pain point, make a suggestion, manage objections, and close the sale. This process was also loaded with complex combinations of products and services where the retailer would identify the Unique Selling Proposition, or USP, of the products, services, and the business relationship.

To draw a connection to Pink's idea, solution sales techniques were ideal for a world of "buyer beware", where retailers knew everything and the customer knew very little. In the NPR interview Pink goes on to say, "Something curious has happened in the last 10 years in that you can walk into a car dealership with the invoice price of the car, something that even the salesmen/women at car dealers didn't know too long ago. And so in a world of information parity, or at least something close to it, we've moved — caveat emptor is still good advice, but equally good advice for the sellers is caveat venditor, seller beware."

One of the hardest things for bike retailers to come to terms with is that customers simply do not need retailers in the way they used to. Hence solutions sales, for the majority of the world, are dead. Customers' needs have changed and the bike retailer is no longer the source of all information. Instead of taking a trip to the IBR and talk with someone for an hour, customers will take out their phone, do a quick search, and get a detailed analysis of the products' USPs, prices, and availability. Owners and managers have seen this first hand as they encounter a growing group of customers who know more about a specific product than anyone working in the store. In some cases the customer knows more about a product than even the manufacturer does.

When customers have this level of information the insight anyone on the retail floor can provide is minimal, and whatever information they do have can be researched and validated on the spot. For the past 150 years of bike retail the smartest person in the room was the person selling the bike. The retailer held all the cards, they knew the technology, they knew the features, the benefits, the availability, and they could bend that information any way they saw fit to achieve the sale. Today, with a smartphone and a solid connection, the customer holds all the cards in the sales process. And it's not just the younger people that are accessing information before they buy. Kevin Kelly, the Senior Maverick at Wired Magazine has said, "65 percent of 55-64 year olds surf, text and watch television simultaneously".[4] Neither the retailer nor the catalogs they stock are the source bike information, the internet is.

The death of Solution Sales will be the unraveling of many bike retailers, they simply won't know, or have the desire to transition. The more agile retailers will move to becoming great leadouts for their customers.

Leadout Method: Approach

Solution Sales teaches to greet customers using open-ended questions that do not relate to business. I believe this is an outdated approach that will only backfire on the majority who try to use it. When someone walks into an IBR they know why they're there; to purchase something. They also believe that the only reason anyone would be working there is to sell them something. So when someone begins a conversation with a question like, "That is a wonderful bag, how do you like it?" or "What did you think of the game last night?" the customer knows exactly what is going on. They know the person on the retail floor is making a lame attempt to break the ice by creating meaningless small talk. They know at any moment they will drop the routine with a Rico Suave transition toward talking about product. For many customers, this type of conversation is not a seen as a service but rather an enormous waste of time. The idea of building a friendship with customers through small talk conversation in antiquated at best. In today's consumer-centric environment retailers do not build friendships first, instead they build respect and trust. And they do that through offering a great product or service while respecting a customer's intelligence and time. The faster the person working takes the conversation to business, the more respectful they're being with the customer and their time.

Instead of any formalized greeting a Leadout will offer an invitation-style approach. And like any other invitation the person who receives it has the freedom to say yes or no. Asking a yes/no question goes against every sales training course in the past 50 years, but not in the Leadout Method. A yes-no question is how invitations work. Here's is an example of a Leadout sending an invitation:

Timmy: Can I help you today?
Customer: No thanks, I'm just looking.

You're probably thinking I made a typo somewhere- I assure you, I did not. When someone is asked a yes/no question the odds are very good they're going to respond with "no". The experts were correct about this 50 years ago and they're still correct today. Solution Sales advocates will preach against this, for them this response is seen as the king of all negatives. They will preach that this approach is completely giving up the sale in the first few moments of engaging the customer. They will teach that once the customer says no, they will keep saying no. I disagree.

This approach works because many customers simply prefer a quiet moment to roam the store, get their bearings, and do a bit of research without interruption. This response is completely acceptable in today's retail because odds are very good the customer has already done a fair amount of research on the product before they walked into the store. With that research done, their need for comfort is now greater than their need for help or a relationship with the retailer.

The goal of the invitation is not to get them to engage, the goal is to make them aware that someone is available to help. However this needs to be done while maintaining control of the conversation. Compare these two examples:

Example 1 (and the more common approach I see)
Timmy: My name is Timmy. Can I help you find anything?
Customer: No thanks, I'm just looking.
Timmy: Ok, I'll be over here, let me know if you need anything.

This approach leaves the customer in a very uncomfortable place. In order for the customer to get help they will have to first, find the employee and, second, consciously or subconsciously admit that they may not know enough to appear as a savvy shopper. This is a feeling no one wants to have before a possible price negotiation.

Example 2 (maintaining control of the conversation)
Leadout: My name is Timmy. Can I help you find anything?
Customer: No thanks, I'm just looking.
Leadout: Ok, I'm going to finish up some work over here. I'll be back in a few minutes to see how you're doing.

In the second example the customer is allowed their free space but any future conversation is in the hands of the Leadout. The customer will never have to find an employee or admit to not knowing something. All they need to do is wait for the Leadout to return. When the customer needs help they will have a question waiting when the Leadout returns.

What if they don't have a question when the Leadout returns? In this scenario the Leadout simply tells them again they will return but now double the time that they will be away. Instead of coming back in a few minutes, they will come back in five. If they're still not ready to talk, they come back in 10. If the customer leaves the store before Leadout can engage, no one should fret. The customer had plenty of time to look through the store, they were given time to do their own research, and they know that the Leadout was there to help if they were ready. This is a very positive impression to have left on this customer. It may not be a full conversion but it is a micro-conversion toward winning them over.

Leadout Method: Research

When the customer is ready to talk it is important to remember that the goal for a Leadout is to gain trust and respect. The vast majority of people walk into an IBR with an intent to buy. The era of window shopping or "I'm just looking" is over. If someone has chosen to get off the couch, get dressed, get into their car or on their bike, travel to the store, and walk through the doorway- they did it for a reason. Consider these statistics:

98% of shoppers read product reviews on retailer or manufacturer websites when considering a higher-end purchase.[5]

40% consult external review websites in their purchase decisions and consumers choosing among higher-end products are more likely to visit external review websites prior to purchasing.[6]

95% of smartphone users have looked for local information. 77% of them contacted the business and 44% purchased.[7]

74% of consumers look to social networks to guide their purchases.[8]

An example I often use in presentations is to ask, "What was the last purchase you made that cost over $500 that was not bike related. Perhaps it was a phone, a piece of furniture, a computer, or even a car. Odds a very good that before you walked into a brick and mortar retailer to purchase this item, you either knew exactly what you were going to buy or you were prepared to purchase if the retailer had an item that worked for you." When someone walks into a bike retailer I believe they are ready to purchase a product. It is just a matter of answering these questions for them.

- Does the retailer have the product or service the customer had in mind, or something similar?

- Is it selling for a price they are comfortable with?

- Is the retailer pleasant and easy to work with?

These, on a macro level, are the questions all customers are looking to have answered. Specific answers about the technical features and benefits should be seen as secondary.

Where many go wrong is assuming that the customer walking in the store knows nothing about cycling or the bike they're looking for. This is not the case. Bicycles are considered a high-cost, low-frequency purchase. Like a phone, a piece of furniture, a computer, or a car- we do not make these purchases very often (low frequency) and they usually cost a good amount of money (high cost).

The higher the cost or the lower the frequency, the more research someone will do on their options. People spend months and sometimes years researching the right home to buy or rent. These types of purchases demand thorough attention and review before making a commitment to buy. Conversely, when purchasing a low cost and high frequency item most people do not dedicate much time researching. Very few are spending hours upon hours researching the best peanut butter. For high frequency and lost cost items people are more likely to perform research through trial and error.

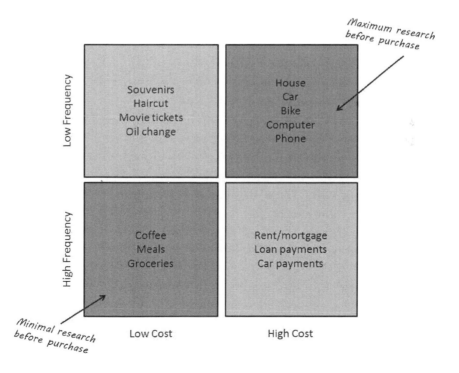

Fig 6.1: Cost versus frequency and their effect on researching goods

Since bicycles sit firmly in the top right of the chart (see Fig 6.1), lower frequency and higher cost, it is a very safe assumption that customers who are standing in a bike retailer have done some research. Which leads to the most powerful and telling question the Leadout can ask, "What research have you done?"

This question that is commonly used when employers are conducting interviews for potential new hires. The question establishes a sense of trust but at the same time will give our Leadout some key information to do their work better. When a customer answers this question they will be providing an understanding of what bikes they've looked at, what shops they've visited, what type of riding they see themselves doing, and even provide a sense of what they're planning to spend. It is one question that will pull dozens of answers. There are three answers in particular that will cover the majority of the responses.

Leadout: What research have you done?
Customer #1: I was looking at a bike at another bike shop.
Customer #2: My friends recommended a bike.
Customer #3: I was researching a bike online.

I will be break down each of these responses and describe how a great Leadout would handle each situation.

Customer #1: I was looking at a bike at another bike shop.
Leadout: Tell me why you didn't buy it?

Customer #2: My friends recommended a bike.
Leadout: Tell me what you do not like about your current bike.

Customer #3: I was researching a bike online.
Leadout: What did you like about the bikes you researched?

The answers to these questions will be magic in the Leadout's hands. The customer will be saying exactly what they want to hear the Leadout say. If they were shopping at another bike shop, and the Leadout asks them why they didn't buy it. They will respond with a very specific list of features and/or benefits. When the leadout presents these features and benefits, the customer will be more likely to make the purchase.

Leadout: Why didn't you buy the bike from them?
Customer: The bike was heavy, they didn't have my size and the saddle was very uncomfortable.

All a Leadout has to do is focus on the list of appropriate features when speaking to the customer. "This bike is light, we have your size, and we have a number of saddles so you can choose the most comfortable one." Solution Sales will teach us to focus on the USP of each product while a Leadout will focus on the USP that is most relevant to the customer. The bike may have the most advanced suspension system or carbon layup ever designed but if the customer is worried about saddle comfort, open the discussion with saddles. This is where many people often make mistakes, instead of focusing on customer concerns, many people boast and show off their knowledge about the bike. Take this example of Timmy on the retail floor:

Timmy: Why didn't you buy the bike from them?
Customer: The bike was heavy, they didn't have my size and the saddle was very uncomfortable.
Timmy: Well this bike is full carbon and uses triple monocoque construction, has Shimano components, ceramic bearing, press fit bottom bracket, and 110mm of travel with independently adjustable rebound and compression.
Customer: (stares blankly) Can I have catalog? I should do some more research.

It was said best in Randy Kirk's Principles of Bicycle Retailing, "If they didn't tell you they had a shifting problem. Why are you talking to them about derailleurs?"[9] This uncontrolled blabbering is what I like to call verbal diarrhea. It is an act of selfishness when people focus on sharing everything they know rather than teaching the customer what they want to learn. Verbal diarrhea happens because many people working in bike retail believe that if they bury the customer in facts and figures they will be overwhelmed by the value and be completely hooked on buying the bike. This couldn't be further from the reality.

Focusing on the customer's interests is the cure to verbal diarrhea. These simple questions will allow a Leadout to understand what the customer has in mind, but it doesn't always mean that the product the customer has chosen will be the best product for the experience. Which is why the final question is the most important, "Can you tell me how you see yourself using this bike?"

Customers will answer this question by defining the most common uses for the bike they're thinking of purchasing. If they have researched a full suspension mountain bike but tell the Leadout how they see themselves using the bike to commute on or take on a sixty mile road ride, then the product they have researched does not align with the intended use. In these rare cases it is the responsibility of the Leadout to explain how the bike is intended to be used and the benefit or detriment of using it another way. The customer may still choose the full suspension mountain bike for the sixty mile road ride, but they will have made that decision after having been informed on why it may not be the best choice.

Leadout Method: Context

At the end of every bike purchase many customers are happy and excited to head out and begin their new lives as cyclists. In their eyes, owning a bike means they have everything they need. However a great Leadout knows they are far from prepared. The customer will still need a helmet, a pair of shoes, cycling shorts, a frame pump, a jersey, a bike fitting, and the list goes on and on.

In many instances the customer came prepared to spend $1000 but they were able to justify buying a bike for more than their budget. Now they are going to have the rude awakening when they learn they still need several hundred more dollars' worth of equipment to ensure they have a safe, worry free and fun cycling experience. For the most experienced staff on the retail floor this moment in the process is awkward. It is especially awkward as they guide the customer around the store and struggle to convince them why they should spend another $50 here and another $100 there. It is a difficult and uncomfortable process for everyone involved. For less confident people working in an IBR, this moment is so awkward that they do not even bother. They sell the bike and stand proud in their ability to move someone from their $1000 budget.

If customers head out the door unprepared they have two very distinct paths ahead, neither of them good for the IBR that sold them the bike. The first path they could take is to ride their bike and have an uncomfortable, painful, and cumbersome experience. They may put up with it for a ride or two but they'll soon start to be more annoyed with the cycling experience that overjoyed. The bike will then find its way to the back of the garage where it will stay. They will never again try cycling and they will never again be a customer.

The second path is for the few customers who are strong enough to push past the initial stage of discomfort and start asking questions. They will ask "Why does it hurt?" or "Why are the tires going flat" or "How do I fit a bike in a car?" They'll learn that there were things they should have purchased and been taught about when they got their bike but for some reason no one in the store told them. Having lost trust, they head over to the other bike shop in town and they will never again be a customer.

To overcome this awkward moment Leadouts need to help customers predict their next purchases. By using a Prediction Card that lists out all the items a new cyclist will need, the Leadout will be helpful, not overbearing. See Fig 6.2 and 6.3.

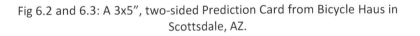

Fig 6.2 and 6.3: A 3x5", two-sided Prediction Card from Bicycle Haus in Scottsdale, AZ.

After the customer has agreed to purchase a bike, the Leadout hands them the customer a Prediction Card and says, "People who have purchased this bike will buy these items within the next 60 days, can I tell you why a floor pump is important?" On average customers who have been given a Prediction Card will purchase 2-3 items from the card, and then use the card as a checklist for future purchases.

Should a customer decide not purchase anything from the Prediction Card the retailer is safe. They have done their job to inform the customer why these items are important, if a customer opts out of purchasing the items on the Prediction Card they have done so as informed consumers. They were never misguided or not told what items they need. If they turn down the suggestion to buy a floor pump and have flat tires three days later, they won't be annoyed with the people who sold them the bike. They will be more annoyed with themselves.

Some bike shops have even taken to showing customers the Prediction Card at the beginning of a bike sale as well. Helping the customer understand everything that is involved and have given them insight on how to spend their money more wisely.

In conclusion, Solution Sales is dead. Insight Sales will take retailers, customers, and the store to a new level of positive experiences. Using the Leadout Method will increase conversion rates, decrease time needed with each customer, and ensure the customer is purchasing the right bike while building trust and respect.

Are You Store #1 or #2?

Are you the first store people go to? Or are you the second? And why does it matter?

The shopping experience in an IBR is drastically different than the shopping experience in nearly every other type of sporting goods retail. Despite the mission statements from Northface, REI, or Lululemon, these retailers are not attempting to have relationship building conversations with their consumers. They're not looking to embrace them and bring them into their community and culture. Their goal for these retailers is to assist the customer in finding the best product(s), creating brand loyalty, and getting them on their way.

A bike retailer is, and has always been, different. People working in IBRs want to build a relationship with the customer, understand their goals, and help connect them to the perfect bike that will set them on a lifelong path in the sport of cycling. Bike retailers want to share their love and passion for the sport. And frankly, today's consumers aren't ready for this level of customer service. This customer service is becoming the outlier and it can catch quite a few people off guard.

When someone visits Store #1 it's a bit of a shock. They're thrown off by the person that wants to connect, understand, and engage. They're so thrown off that they leave so they can regroup and gather their thoughts. Some customers give up on the idea, some go and shop online, but the determined few press on. Those few are hell-bent on getting themselves a bicycle.

In comes the Store #2. The customer isn't going to return to Store #1, because that would be embarrassing. Now that they understand how this retailer/customer relationship is going to work, they've rehearsed what they're going to say, they're ready to answer the big questions, and they walk into Store #2 prepared and ready to engage.

The small goal is to be Store #2 more than Store #1. The big goal is to be Store #1 *and* #2.

Embrace the Testers

Any time someone ventures into cycling for the first time the purchase will always be frugal. Instead of spending $2000 on the bike they probably need, they'll spend $500 on a bike just to test the waters.

People do this type of product testing with everything they buy. They start out by buying the cheap shoes, which are uncomfortable and wear out too quickly. From then on, they're happy to invest in a pair of shoes at five times the price. They buy the cheap speakers, but the sound sucks, so they come back to buy the nicer ones. They buy cheap shampoo, but it damages their hair, then they buy the more expensive shampoo.

When people start anything they start small, determine their style and preferences, then come back and buy what they feel is best for them. This is the human element of how people shop. Retailers should not try to fight or ignore it, instead they should embrace it.

Instead of pushing someone toward buying a $2000 bike retailers should be comfortable selling them a $500 bike, all the needed accessories, a membership for a cycling club, a free course in beginner cycling, and attending the Wednesday night shop ride to them meet other cyclists. A week later the leadout can email a list of maintenance tips and send out regular tweets about upcoming events.

This is the type of customer service many retailers normally reserve for their highest dollar customers. However, when given to someone who purchased the cheapest bike on the retail floor they will be dedicated customers for life. When it comes time for a second bike, it is very likely they will not settle for a $2000 bike. They'll be buying a $5,000 bike this time.

Speaking Multiple Languages

The majority of a retailer's time is spent communicating with others yet basic communication skills are often taken for granted. It is no surprise that the difficulty with communication is at the core of many arguments, disagreements, or worse- lost sales. Here are my quick tricks any retailer can use to become a better communicator.

First, words and phrases that seem perfectly acceptable to someone working on the retail floor can be off-putting or even offensive for customers. One tactic is to avoid language that steers the conversation toward negativity or disagreement. This type of language Kung Fu helps to ease the customer's worry and shows empathy. Here is a chart running through some of the more common communications bike retailers will have.

When discussing:	Avoid	Use
Mechanical issues	Broken Failure F---ed Snapped Weird	Not working as it should There is an issue...
Price	Expensive A lot Cheap Not cheap Discounted The best we can do is... Today's price is... The sale price is...	The price is... It is priced at
Something not covered by warranty	Unfortunately Too bad it's... Sucks to be you	As it turns out
When the customer is incorrect	You're wrong It doesn't work that way We can't/don't do that	I recommend using it like... Let me explain how I can help... I understand and can help by...
Repairs	We fixed We solved Shouldn't be a problem	I would like you to test it It worked in all our tests We reduced the rubbing/clanking
When you feel a customer chooses incorrectly	This isn't the right one for you That doesn't go with that I wouldn't do that	What do you think about... Can I tell you why others choose...

Second is body language, another way retailers can communicate with customers. The goal of reading or communicating with body language is to make the customer as comfortable as possible. It will be important for those on the retail floor to read the customer's body language but at the same time be aware of their own.

144

Negative body language
Moving or leaning away from you
Crossed arms or legs
Moving away to the side
Feet pointed away from you
Feet pointed toward the exit
Rubbing or scratching face/neck

Negative body language
Moving or leaning closer to you
Relaxed, uncrossed limbs
Long periods of eye contact
Nodding
Tilting head to the side

Scared to purchase
Starring at or touching price tag
Not touching bike
Looking around the store
Staring at floor

Ready to purchase
Kneeling by bike
Touching bike
Lifting or leaning on the bike

With these simple tricks retailers can eliminate many of the communication hurdles that others fumble through.

Customers Shopping Online

I am often asked how to handle customers who showroom an IBR. Showrooming is when someone will use a bike retailer to answer questions about sizing, what components are needed, what upgrades would be recommended, and even test ride a bike; then they buy it elsewhere, usually online. This can be frustrating for many owners and managers. Here are the common questions I get about showrooming and my responses.

If they buy it online, should we charge more to build it? A retailer can do this, but I would recommend to first change the mindset and vocabulary. We should never punish customers for buying elsewhere, which is the customer's right in a free marketplace. If an IBR punishes customers for being budget conscious, they will rebel by never working with that retailer on anything and may even begin telling their riding buddies why. Notice that I do not differentiate between purchasing online or purchasing at a competing local bike shop. If the money didn't end up in the cash drawer, it doesn't matter where it was spent.

Instead of punishing customers who do not buy, I encourage retailers to reward customers that do. It's a small switch in mindset and vocabulary but a powerful one that can create community and loyalty. Airlines do this all the time- the more flights people buy with any airline, the better they are rewarded.

As an example, an IBR can inflate their service prices by 15% across the board and then say, "All service work on bikes purchased from Donny's Bike Shop is 15% cheaper than our standard pricing". This has two winning sides for the IBR. First, people who buy elsewhere but choose to have the service work done will be paying more on average. Second, when selling a bike the retailer can leverage this as value-added against any requests for discounts. They may say something like, "I'm sorry, we do not offer a discount on this bike but you should know that by purchasing with us you will save 15% on every repair for the life of the bike."

The next evolution of this is to have premier packages for premier customers. For example: "Our Donny's Bike Shop Carbon Club is for customers who purchase more than $8000 worth of product from us in a calendar year. Carbon Club members receive same day service and delivery on all repairs." This creates a sense of elite-level belonging for those that can afford it. It could also help everyone on the retail floor by giving them tools to move buyers from a $6000 bike to an $8000 bike.

How do I stop customers from buying online? This is difficult because the internet will offer something a brick and mortar retailer never can. The internet will always have the best prices and the widest selection. That is a very attractive offer not dissimilar to when someone purchases airline tickets online versus going to a travel agent. To get someone to shop with a brick and mortar retailer means finding a true differentiator. If a customer can save $1000 by purchasing online, what really makes the brick and mortar retailer $1000 better? Many bike retailers think return

146

policies, warranty, or being assured of getting an undamaged bike in the right size is enough to win the sale, but often it is not. Many riders will sacrifice these things- to them it is a calculated risk they are willing to take in order to save money.

A retailer's point of differentiation is for them to find, no one can give it to them. It's best when the differentiator is something other IBRs cannot replicate. One tactic I've seen work well is to bring new riders into a cultivated community of cyclists to ride with. "By purchasing at Donny's Bike Shop you are part of the Donny's Bike Shop family. We have four club rides each week, one social night every month, a free 6-month training plan, and you will receive a free 30-minute consultation with a local cycling coach. We sell annual memberships to this club for $2000, but it's only $200 with the purchase of a bike and free with the purchase of a bike over $8000"

However, many bike retailers have not cultivated any value in their community- it's not a selling point yet. No one cares about joining a community if there are only 3 people in it.

Another tactic is to sell sizing and bike fitting first. If someone is looking at a bike online and researching with a brick and mortar retailer, I would encourage the retailer to sell the bike fitting first. Plenty of horror stories out there of people purchasing the wrong bike size and getting stuck. On the retail floor one might try this: "A bike sizing costs $50 and is fully refunded when a bike is purchased at Donny's Bike Shop. A Body Geometry Fit costs $300 and the team at Donny's Bike Shop will help you by writing a prescription for any additional pieces you may need for the bike you purchase; such as a stem, handlebars, saddles, cables, bar tape, pedals, and labor work. On average this saves $300 in trial and error." The more items on that list that come from manufacturers who do not sell online, the better chance the brick and mortar retailer can garner the sale.

How do I know if customers are showrooming me? Easy, just ask. "Have you researched this bike online at all?" or even more bluntly, "Are you planning to buy the bike here or online?" When someone is showrooming odds are good they have already committed to purchasing somewhere else. Instead of fretting over the bike sale, retailers should think of it as an opportunity to win the additional sales like fitting, repair, accessories, and apparel by acting as their consultant and helping them with their online purchase.

Chapter 6
Vansevenant Checklist

Change the approach on the retail floor. It is ok to ask a yes/no question as long as you maintain control of the conversation.

Start asking what research people have done.

Create a checklist of items people will need when they purchase a bike.

Embrace people who are only testing your product. Not every person will be a conversion. Some will only be micro conversions.

Sit down with your staff and talk about words to use and not use.

Discuss how you can read your customer's body language.

Welcome showrooming by offering truly differentiated services.

7

Marketing the IBR

"Why do retailers need real-time information? Would anyone riding a bike want to make a left hand turn on a highway based on a snapshot taken 15 minutes ago?
- Frank Andryauskas

Merriam-Webster defines marketing as "The activities that are involved in making people aware of a company's products, making sure that the products are available to be bought, etc." I would confidently say that this is the most boring definition of marketing I have ever read. Instead I believe that effective marketing- unlike advertising or branding -means only doing two things.

1. Maintain a positive connection with customers.
2. Be extremely helpful.

When a woman walks into her local IBR and gets treated poorly she will tell her friends and campaign against that store. This is marketing. When a man buys a bike and loses 40 pounds his colleagues will start asking him how he did it. This is marketing. If a retailer sells an inferior product and it breaks within the first week of using it. This is also marketing. Marketing is completely baked into every aspect of a business, the products sold, and how people are treated. It is important to remember that the most powerful and lasting marketing anyone could ever do is maintaining the positive connection with customers while being extremely helpful.

Word of Mouth Marketing

In a room of over one hundred IBRs I asked what they thought the best form of marketing was. Almost the entire group agreed that word-of-mouth marketing was the best for their businesses, and I agree. However, word-of-mouth marketing can be very difficult to track and even more difficult to cultivate. How does a retailer get someone to talk about a shopping experience? How will they know if it ever happens? How do retailers know if their customers conveyed the vision of the business in the same way the retailer would have? While many people understand that word-of-mouth marketing is the most valuable to the business it can be a difficult beast to capture.

What if I said there was a magical tool that allowed all IBRs to create effective word-of-mouth marketing strategies? What if I also said that this tool could track how people talk about any shopping and cycling experience and, even better, allowed the IBR to join in on the conversation at any moment? And what if I said that the tool was very inexpensive or even free, all it will take is dedicating a few hours a week? Any retailer should want to use this magical tools right? These tools exist and they are called Facebook, Twitter, Instagram, and Strava.

These social tools are the new backbone of every marketing plan from Fortune 500 businesses to a garage start-up. They allow retailers to track word-of-mouth marketing and create a direct connection to customers. Writing about social channels can be a bit dangerous, there is a very real possibility that any of the social channels I mentioned above may not be around five years from now. Nevertheless, the ideas of how we can use social will be here for a very long time. Social has, in every way, rewritten the way businesses engage with their customers. As of this writing here are the activity levels of the four most useful channels for an IBR.

Facebook: 1.3 billion monthly active users. (1/1/14)[1]

Twitter: 645 million registered users. (1/1/14)[2]

Instagram: 152 million users. (11/17/13)[3]

Strava: 3.5 million accounts created (1/3/14)[4]

These social channels are viewed by many small businesses as a Godsend. This is because they can achieve so much with so little investment. It's no secret, IBRs don't have the largest marketing budget. On average an IBR will dedicate 2-3% of their total revenue to marketing efforts. In a half million dollar business that means only $10,000 to $15,000 to dedicate toward marketing. A budget that size can be eaten up entirely by sponsoring a cycling club. Knowing that the average cost of a primetime television ad is over $100,000, traditional marketing efforts like television, radio, and print are not an option for many bike retailers. This is where the power of social steps in.

Time and Money on Social

Where should a retailer start? It is easy to get confused by the vast amount of choices. Choices like Facebook ads, promoted tweets, search engine optimization, ad redirecting, and content creation. There are many ways a retailer could invest their time and money on social channels and someone could push themselves to institutionalization trying to comprehend all of them. We are still in the very early days of online marketing and everyone is pushing the boundaries for what can be done. In terms of age the internet is a college student. Facebook, Twitter, and YouTube haven't even hit puberty yet and Instagram is still wearing diapers. The world of social is constantly shifting and that change can be intimidating

While the platforms may be young, it is more important than ever to be involved. In his book Jab, Jab, Jab, Right Hook social media consultant Gary Vaynerchuk draws a comparison between social platforms and boxing.[5] He points out that a great boxer could never have had success if they only threw a right hook. They also could have never won a fight by only throwing jabs. Boxers have to use a combination of punches. Jabs break an opponent down while a right hook is meant to lay them out for the count. In terms of social, Vaynerchuk believes that many businesses are only throwing right hooks, others are only throwing jabs, and a very select few are effectively boxing.

Here are the four areas a bike retailer could invest their time and money in social to become an effective social boxer.

Promotion (right hook). This is how far too many IBRs use social media; look at us, check out our sale, come to our event, and buy our stuff.

Perhaps "social media" is a bad name, because too many people seem to focus on the word "media". Facebook, Twitter, Instagram, etc is not the place for advertising. These are social channels, not media channels. As such, people do not want their feeds cluttered with a retailer's announcement that helmets are 20% off. It is important to have an element of promotion, but too much becomes intrusive and a bike retailer will lose more credibility than they could gain. I recommend to save promotions for the final round- after having laid out some quality jabs.

Contextual conversation (jab). Imagine being at a party and overhearing two people talking about cycling. What should a retailer in this situation say? Should they ignore them? Should they interrupt yell "We have a mega-sale this weekend!", or should they simply join the conversation. Any right-minded person would of course, do the latter. Social media is millions of people having a conversation.

When World Champion Evelyn Steven's updates her Twitter none of her followers feel special. Anyone can update their status and tossing up a post about a race she did doesn't mean she is having a conversation with anyone. If Evelyn's followers hit the Favorite button or reply with comments- this still isn't a conversation. Still, no one feels really special.

However, when Evelyn writes, responds, and engages with her audience people will start to feel really special. Even if all she says is thank you, this is a conversation. If Evelyn goes as far as writing a well thought out response then people will feel amazingly connected to her. They will be able to say, "I was chatting with the World Champion and...".

An IBR can do the same thing by setting a goal to respond to every comment, tweet, and post. This may sound like a lot, but speaking to someone through social is no different than speaking to them face-to-face when they are standing in the store.

Customer service (jab, jab). Social channels are where customers can connect with the IBRs they love, ask questions, or complain about service. Providing amazing customer service is crucial to any social strategy. Before social channels, if someone was upset with a retailer they had a likelihood of telling 10-12 people. Today they will tell thousands of people within a few seconds.

Twitter tends to be the primary channel people use to ask questions, get advice, or complain about a business. This is because Twitter, unlike Facebook, does not require making a connection before beginning a conversation. If someone wants to talk to an acquaintance, celebrity, or IBR they can jump on Twitter and immediately call them out. Calling a company's 800-number to get customer service could take hours whereas a post on Twitter usually gets a response within minutes.

In 2012 Adam Jackson rented out his apartment using the service AirBnB.com and the guests who stayed in his home stole his pizza cutter. Jackson took to Twitter and told all of his followers about the missing pizza cutter and tagged AirBnB in the post. AirBnB realized that if Jackson continued to have items stolen every time he rented out his apartment, eventually he would get frustrated and stop using their service. To alleviate this the AirBnB Customer Service team overnighted a brand new pizza cutter to Jackson with a note saying, "Dear Adam, We heard your pizza cutter went missing. We love pizza and we love you too. Enjoy!" This response led Jackson to repost the story, which was then shared all over the world as a lesson for how one company offers amazing service. AirBnB never guessed that buying a pizza cutter would turn into some of their best marketing. They were simply taking steps to save a relationship by offering great customer service.

Not every post on Twitter will require a retailer to replace something for free. Most complaints can be handled with a polite and empathetic line of communication, but it is important to have a budget dedicated to solving problems. If a customer has a new tire and tube installed, gets a flat tire later that day, and complains about it on Twitter- that could be the retailer's chance to go above and beyond. Either installing a new tube for free or even sending someone to their home to do the installation there. Done correctly, bad experiences can be turned into some of the most powerful marketing.

Gratitude (jab, jab, jab). If someone walked into their local IBR in 1995 and purchased a mountain bike the retailer would have very limited knowledge about this person. All they would really know is that the customer sees themselves as a mountain biker, the customer's address and phone number, but that is about it. In this mid-90s example, the retailer has no real idea of who their customers are. If they wanted to thank this person for their patronage with a small gift the best they could probably muster up is a water bottle or book on mountain biking. The gift would have been a nice gesture, but that retailer would never know if the customer really enjoyed it.

Gratitude is the bulk of a retailer's social agenda. Using social effectively will allow IBRs to mine an incredibly specific amount of data from their customers. For example, if anyone were to follow my social feeds (@donnyperry) they would learn I have two dogs, I enjoy having Mexican food with my girlfriend, watch superhero movies, drink bourbon, listen to business podcasts, and travel frequently. With a couple minutes of study anyone could have very specific details about me and that specificity would allow them to cater to me in very unique ways. If a retailer sent me the Captain America themed dog dish for my pups as a congratulations gift for a recent promotion I got at work, I would be their customer for life.

Gratitude can be simple too. Should a retailer stumble across an article about a new winery opening up they could forward that article and tag customers who they know love wine. Maybe even suggest a weekend ride followed by a tasting.

154

By focusing time and budget on showing gratitude to the customers, retailers will be achieving the two goals of great marketing; maintaining a positive connection and being extremely helpful.

Only 3 Customers

In my view, there are only three people who could walk into an IBR. These three customers are not determined by their locality, age, gender, or any other demographic.

Customer 1: Cyclists in your market who have purchased from you before.

Customer 2: Cyclists in your market who have not purchased from you.

Customer 3: People in your market who are not cyclists.

Thinking about customers in these three categories helps retailers understand where to invest their time, money, and energy. Most business owners want the best return for the least amount of effort. Many consultants will say that the big money is with new customer acquisition (Customer 2 and 3), and they are correct. A new customer will bring a lot of money. Especially Customer 3 because this is a customer that has never been a cyclist before and they likely need one of everything; a new bike, helmet, shoes, clothing, etc.

What the consultant may forget to mention is that the costs of acquiring Customer 3 is astronomical and for a small business and can bury them in debt. To break it down:

Customer 3: People in your market who are not cyclists. These potential customers are the most difficult to get in the doors. Since they have never been a cyclist, an IBR will have the added challenge of convincing them to take up an entirely new sport. This requires a massive marketing effort to put the IBR in front of people who are likely to start cycling. Perhaps they'll focus on runners or yogis or CrossFit athletes; but in each case they'll be asking them to move away from a sport they are already invested in and into a sport that is not currently on their radar. The costs here are baffling and the return on investment is so low that any IBR that takes this route is likely to go out of business long before they garner enough customers to pay the bills.

Customer 2: Cyclists in your market who have not purchased from you. If there is a cyclist who has not purchased from a local bike retailer we can deduce that they are purchasing their bikes and gear somewhere else. Be it at another IBR or through an online retailer. However they are buying, they trust the channel they're purchasing through enough to not give any other retailer a try.

So what is the strategy for getting this customer to move away from their current shopping pattern and start shopping somewhere new? First the IBR will need to market to them through the same channels as the competition. Second, they will need to create content or host events that will draw their attention. Third, they will need to show the customer why they are a better choice and fourth, provide an easy path for the customer to follow from wherever they are to the bike retailer's front door. It is costly, time consuming, and since Customer 2 usually has everything they need as a cyclists, the payoff rarely trumps the investment.

Customer 1: Cyclists in your market who have purchased from you before. There is an old school lesson is sales that says, "The best time to get someone to buy something is after they've bought something." This lesson still holds true today.

Someone who has already purchased from a local bike retailer is already a cyclist, they trust that retailer enough to have given them money, they know where they're located and they understand the type of services they offer. Getting this person back in the door is the easiest conversion of all. Ideally they are already in the scope of the current marketing and participate in the retailer's community of cyclists. The strategy with this person, or group of people, is to increase contextual conversation and gratitude. Reach out to them on a regular basis, tell them about upcoming events, host their club rides, and have an understanding for what they want to achieve in the sport. Then express genuine gratitude. This can be done with a simple email, phone call, or hand shake. It can also be done with customer appreciation parties, frequent purchase programs, or even gifts.

Investing time and money in customer 1 will yield the highest rewards.

Who and How

Many IBRs struggle to find the right person to manage social engagement. This is a common hurdle that many IBRs face. Commonly the answer is to find the person who is the most digitally inclined and hand over the keys of the throne to them. More often than not, this meant that the entire online presence was being managed by one of the youngest staff members. While this isn't necessarily bad, it may not be good either.

If thousands of customers were standing outside the front door who should go outside and talk to them? Odds are, a retailer would want everyone in the store to head outside or at the very least the best people to represent the business. Social channels are the primary form of communication coming from any business. They will engage more people per day than will ever come through the doors. This is why the people who should manage social channels should be the best trained, most knowledgeable, and most effective communicators in the business. Just because Timmy regularly posts to Instagram does not mean that he should manage the Instagram feed for a business.

Five years ago, for a large majority of IBRs, this type of work wasn't even considered important. Today it is what separates an IBR from their competition. Today people looking for a bike shop will reach into their pocket, pull out their phone, and do a Google search for "bike shop". When the results pop up only 2-3 shops will appear in the screen and the rest will require them to scroll down. If this is the number one way people find a bike retailer, one of the biggest questions any retailer should have is, how do I make it to the top of Google's list?

A decade ago the answer was search engine optimization, or SEO, where the focus was placed on creating the right keywords on the webpage and having a lot of websites linking to the business' site. While these are important they are dwarfed by the value social platforms will place on Google searches.

Many companies have moved away from having one person who manages their social platforms. It is just becoming too much work. Instead, they are opting to have everyone take a role in engaging with their customers. The idea is that if they are good enough to talk to the customers face-to-face they might have the talents to talk to customers online as well. Just make sure they're using spellcheck.

Once a retailer has determined who should be communicating to the customers, they will have to set standards for how they communicate. If it weren't complicated enough channels like Facebook, Twitter, Instagram, and Strava should not be seen as the same. People use them differently and people communicate on them differently. Each channel requires a different style, voice, and tone in order to appear native to the platform. Vaynerchuk put it best in Jab, Jab, Jab, Right Hook when he said, "You can't just repurpose old material created for one platform, throw it up on another one, and then be surprised when everyone yawns in your face. No one would ever think it was a good idea to use a print ad for a television commercial, or confuse a banner ad for a radio spot. Like their traditional media platform cousins, every social media platform has its own language."

Along with language each platform has its own functional rules. Twitter users know there is nothing more annoying than when someone tweets a link to their Facebook page or to a photo on Instagram. It requires the reader leave the Twitter app and open another. Similarly when someone posts a link on Instagram the IG users just nod their head in frustration because it can't be opened or even copied.

Taking the four languages I discussed; gratitude, promotion, contextual conversation, and customer service and combining them with the four social channels I believe are most relevant to bike retailers I have established how time and budget will be spent on each platform. See fig 7.1.

	Facebook	Twitter	Instagram	Strava
Gratitude	50%	20%	20%	40%
Promotion	12.5%	10%	10%	10%
Contextual Conversation	12.5%	35%	70%	40%
Customer Service	25%	35%	0%	10%

Fig 7.1: How time and budget should be split within each social platform.

It is important to discuss each platform, what language to use, and any of the functional structures that retailers might need to be aware of.

Facebook

Facebook is a monster. With 1.3 billion people, it has the most users of any social platform. 624 million people log onto Facebook on any given day[7] and recent studies have shown that one in five US page views are to Facebook.[8] I want to repeat that to accentuate the weight of my tone, one in five pages visited are to Facebook! In a study posted on The Social Habit 60% of people 12 and older open Facebook right after they wake up and a similar percentage open Facebook right before they go to sleep.[9] Metrics like this prove that Facebook isn't just a channel, but a layer that sits over everything we do. Hence, it is crucial that every IBR should have a Facebook Page for their store so anyone can engage with the business.

The average user will like 4-5 Facebook Pages, which means an IBR will be competing with these other pages for the attention of their fans. To make sure someone's Facebook feed isn't buried in marketing from brands, Facebook gives three different options for posting: organic posts, targeted posts, and sponsored stories.

Organic posts. If a retailer updates their store's Facebook status without paying for it in any way or choosing a demographic for it to be aimed at, this is an organic post. Most of the content I see being posted from IBRs is organic posting. An organic post can have as low as 3% reach to the total fan base.[10] In that scenario, if an IBR has 1000 fans, only 30 people are going to be reading the content on their Facebook feed. In order for an organic post to reach more people it has to be amazing content that will inspire those 30 people to comment, like, and share.

Targeted posts. If a bike retailer wants to speak only to men, aged 35-55, who graduated from university, and live in San Francisco, California; they can do that. By targeting posts retailers can create multiple pieces of content each day and speak to that demographic in a way that will resonate with them. For example, if a retailer wanted to share a photo of a pro downhiller throwing a tail whip but all of their customers who ride DH are under 30, why would they clutter the Facebook feed of everyone over 30? Retailers can also change the language in the post to be more aligned with the riders. A post directed to women could read, "Here is a question for you ladies…."

The more people who engage with an IBR on Facebook, the more Facebook is going to allow that retailer to reach a larger pieces of their fan base. Targeted posts help retailer do that by filtering the posts to the people who are most likely to engage with the content.

Sponsored stories. If a retailer wants to guarantee more people see their content sponsored stories will allow them to purchase more viewership. Let's imagine that Timmy Likes a sponsored story about an upcoming race. Now that story will pop up in all of Timmy's friends' feeds and read "Timmy liked the Upcoming Race".

Sponsored stories are better than Facebook ads (the little boxed advertisements on the right of the page) because they will show up in a mobile device and they are endorsed by a friend. Using sponsored stories does increase a retailer's chance of viewership but only if the content is good to begin with. If the content is crap, it doesn't matter how much the retailer is willing to pay. It won't be liked, commented on, or shared.

To determine which posts are the best ones to promote using sponsored stories, I recommend starting by looking at successful organic and targeted posts. The most popular and engaged posts are the ones that are potentials for a sponsored story.

Once a retailer has determined which Facebook medium to post in (organic, targeted, or sponsored stories), the next step is to determine the most effective timing and tone for the message.

Timing. To win at Facebook retailers want to post regularly and in different mediums. I encourage 1-3 posts per day with some posts being text, others photos, videos, or links. Some studies have shown that weekends will grab the most engagement from fans, the highest traffic days are Thursday and Friday, 1:00pm gets more clicks and 3:00pm gets more shares.[11] However this shouldn't discourage anyone from posting at other times as well, 60% of people will open Facebook before they get out of bed in the morning.[12]

Ultimately a retailer has to choose the best time for to post for their customers. In Tucson people will wake up as early as 3:00am to ride, avoiding the daytime heat so a 3:15 pre-ride Facebook post might make sense. Meanwhile in Minneapolis odds are better that people ride in the middle and hottest part of the day. They could post in the early afternoon to reach the Minnesotan cyclists. Los Angeles retailers may find that posting during rush hour is pointless because people are busy driving their cars whereas New York retailers could post during rush hour with the likelihood that their customers are riding the train home. Every retailer should test different times and days to post, learning when their customers engage.

Tone: Remember Vaynerchuk's definition of a jab versus a right hook? When retailers post about a product that is in stock or on sale, this is a right hook that should have had several jabs come before it. Bike retailers will make the most of their time when they incorporate some story telling that inspires people to think, click, share, or comment.

Poor tone: We have a new shipment of locks, c'mon down and check them out. Starting at $30!!

Great tone: If you have ever had a bike stolen you know the pain and anger people feel. Be sure to lock your bikes everyone.

When people respond to this post it will give the retailer a chance to make a personal connection and talk to them about locks. Remember the goal is conversation which means retailer speaks, the customer responds, and then the retailer speaks again, making a connection.

Poor tone: Register now for our trainer classes! Bring your bike and work up a sweat; Wednesdays @ 7pm, starting 10/23!
Great tone: Indoors or outdoors, where will you be riding this winter?

Everyone who rides indoors should know about the upcoming trainer classes. Everyone who rides outdoors should know about fenders, jackets, and how to winterize their bike. This use of tone first segments the audience and sets them up for a great, personal connection.

Poor tone: Follow us on twitter @Donnysbikeshop? Now might be a good time! We are running a contest to win a TiGr titanium lock. Head over there now!

If someone is reading this on Facebook, they are engaging through Facebook. Asking someone to switch platforms so they can continue to engage is silly, they are already engaging. It would have been better to create a contest on Facebook as well.

Facebook Pre-Post Checklist

Since bike retailers want their Facebook content to be constantly engaging and occasionally inspiring people to act, I have designed a pre-post checklist to use before posting content.

Is the text too long? Keep the writing short, a post below 250 characters can net 60% more engagement and a retailer can even get up to 66% more engagement if they cut it down to less than 80 characters.

Is it provocative, entertaining, or surprising? If the content isn't one of these things then it will not be engaging. And if it isn't engaging the fan base then the retailer is wasting both their time and their customers.

Is the photo striking and high quality? Photos will have a 39% higher engagement rate. If the framing works square photos are best as they will show without cropping on a laptop screen and take up the most real estate on a mobile device. Photos should be a high quality and convey a sense of emotion, movement, and/or humor.

Is the logo or product visible? A photo of a gorgeous line of singletrack may be beautiful but if that photo were to be shared, at a quick glance how would someone know it came from an IBR? Retailers should take the time to overlay their logo or better, show bikes they sell in action with the product logo visible.

Is the call to action clear and in the right place? Every post should be prefaced by asking, what do you want people to do? Comment on it? Tag someone in it? Open a link? Buy something? Retailers should we weary not to bury or confuse the call to action. I recommend only one call to action per post and placing the call to action as early as possible within that post.

Is the post interesting in any way, to anyone? Retailers need to be honest with themselves here, if the post isn't interesting then they shouldn't be cluttering their customers feed with it. Remember the second rule of marketing is to be extremely helpful.

Are you asking too much of the person who is consuming the content? When posting a link the goal is to state a quick opinion or call to action and then have the reader click the link. It is not the time to write 300 characters of thought or have two different calls to action. Keep posts simple and easy to follow.

Twitter

Twitter is easily the second most used social platform with over 645 million accounts and 135,000 more people signing up every day.[13] It could easily carry the moniker "real time social networking site" and is proven as such with hundreds of news programs referring to tweets as near-legitimate sources. Daniel Tosh will live chat on Twitter during his show Tosh.0. Dana White, the president of the UFC will be furiously tweeting during a UFC match. Scott Simon is a host on NPR and used Twitter to post messages from his mother's bedside during her final moments. People spoke of his tweets as they felt they were "humanizing death" and "a moving commentary on death and the elderly".[14] Twitter has quickly grown to be the truest pulse of what is happening in any business or marketplace.

Where the focus of Facebook should be heavier on content than context, Twitter is just the opposite. The context is just as important as the content. This means that Twitter is not always the best platform to schedule tweets unless retailers can predict what will be relevant to their readers in the future.

To win at Twitter retailers need to have a great tone, just as they would with any other channel, but they also have to be timely to what is happening in the community. The easiest way to do this is to follow the trends and add insight for the readers. This does not mean announcing what is happening in the world on Twitter, that is what everyone else will be doing. Adding commentary, insight, flavor, or an idea to a trending topic is a brilliant way to garner some attention for the store and separate from the competition. Trending topics can be current events, businesses, celebrities, ideas, or memes.

Tweets are a constant stream of content on a readers feed. If a retailer wants to stay within their range of scrolling when their readers open the app they'll have to be ready to post 3-8 times a day. Luckily, not every tweet needs to be artfully curated masterpieces like they should be on other platforms. Simply get online and share.

For better viewership on Twitter IBRs can promote tweets. This feature is a pay service that will put a tweet at or near the top of feeds. Retailers can localize a promoted tweet and even set it to speak to a specific demographic.

Replies are about connection. Gary Vaynerchuk has over one million followers on Twitter and the social media maven happily responds to every tweet he gets. The scorecard of a great twitter feed will have a large amount of replies. This is where customer loyalty, respect, and trust are won.

Time flies on Twitter. Replying more than 24 hours after someone has connected with a retailer can be perceived as being ignored and in worse cases an omission of guilt. After connecting with a brand 42% of people expect a response within an hour.[15] Retailers should dedicate a few minutes, two or three times every day to open their Twitter feed and respond to their customers.

Retweets are about reach. In early spring of 2013 Toby Hockley was riding his bike through Norfolk, England when he was clipped by the side view mirror of a car. He was launched from his bike into the hedges on the side of the road. As he picked himself up he realized that the driver did not stop. Hockley was not going to report the hit and run, while it was unfortunate he was not injured and after making a few roadside repairs was able to finish his ride.

At the same time the driver, Emma Way, got on Twitter and posted what she later referred to as the worst mistake of her life, "Definitely knocked a cyclist off his bike earlier. I have right of way - he doesn't even pay road tax!" Her tweet was retweeted hundreds of times and quickly made its way to the feed of the local police department, who brought Way in for questioning and had her charged. She was found guilty by the courts in November of 2013.[16]

When retweeting a funny tweet, a powerful tweet, and in Way's case a stupid tweet, one can have much further reach than the author's direct followers. One goal for an IBR is to create tweets that hit the perfect balance of context and content to get massive retweets and reach out to readers they wouldn't normally be able to.

Twitter Pre-Post Checklist

Before a retailer composes their next 140 character call to action, run through this checklist will help ensure they are set up for success.

Is it to the point? The nature of Twitter is about being succinct. I prefer to keep my character total to less than 100 so that retweets do not require editing and allow my readers some room to make commentary of their own.

Is the hashtag unique and memorable? We will cover hashtags more in a bit but for now remember that not all hashtags are created equal. Find one that stands out.

Is the image attached high quality? Just because it is Twitter and the character count is limited, that doesn't give license to throw in low resolution photos or photos that do not carry the proper tone.

Does the voice sound authentic? Posting "New bib shorts in the store, hurry up and get yours today. [link]" sounds far too corporate for most IBRs. Instead trying something like, "These bib shorts are amazing. So comfy we're wearing them even if we're not cycling. [link]"

Instagram

Instagram is the new kid on the block in the social channel world. Founded in 2010 and acquired by Facebook in the spring of 2012, the photo and video sharing app boasts an impressive 152 million monthly active users and 55 million photos being shared every day.[17] Though for many retailers, using Instagram as a channel has been confusing. Primarily because the photo cannot be shared by others within the platform does not allow for links leading to a product or service page. So why should we even bother with Instagram?

I like to think of Instagram as the store's personal photo magazine. It is a place where people go to be inspired and entertained. Like a photo magazine the photography is important, no one would want to read a magazine that posted image after image of bikes on sale. Instead they would prefer to read a magazine filled with images of people riding, cycling art, and exotic locations to ride. All of them with a classy filter that makes the photo pop.

In October of 2012 video blogger Casey Neistat posted a short video teaching people how to effectively use Instagram,[18] his favorite social media platform. Neistat believes that "If Facebook is Lucky Charms, Instagram is just the marshmallows." The rest of the world seems to agree with Neistat as photo sharing on Instagram is poised to best Twitter in mobile engagement. In his video Neistat goes on to teach us his rules for Instagram, which I will expand on.

It's not about the pictures, it's about sharing. Picture quality is not as important as it is on Facebook or Twitter, but the filter selection on Instagram is impressive in its ability to turn the simplest photos into art. While using no filter is the most popular choice among Instagrammers, the Mayfair filter has resulted in the most engagement for users, followed by Inkwell and Walden.[19] For brands the most popular filter choice was Lofi and Valencia, the lesson we can take from this- use filters.[20]

The best tip I can offer anyone using Instagram filters is to keep filter use to a minimum. I prefer choosing only one image enhancement feature at a time.

Find your theme and share it. It is very easy to expand too wide with Instagram. Retailers will want to post photos of bikes in the store, bikes they're working on, the technician's new mustache, and the newest box from the vendor. A scattered focus on Instagram does not result in focused attention. Instead retailers should pick a theme that will resonate with their customers and stick to it. For most IBRs that theme will be cycling. Photos of people riding and experiencing life from behind the handlebars.

This is a challenge because many people working in an IBR are working for 50 hours each week, when are they supposed to get out and experience life on a bike so they can effectively Instagram it? Easy, they don't. When they can't ride and take photos of their own they can follow their customers' feeds, copy, and repost their best photos (with their permission of course). Reposting photos can be done by taking a screenshot of their post or better, by having the customer send the original. Whenever reposting, one should always be sure to give credit to photographer.

Easy with the hashtags. Neistat tells us to take it easy with the hashtags. I say, as long as the hashtags are creative and relevant to the photo, go for it. Brands with under 1000 followers saw significantly more interactions when they used 11 hashtags. Not sure why the magic number is 11, it just is.[22]

Post one picture, then chill. The absolute worst thing a retailer can do is post 2, 3, 4, or more photos in a row. Post a photo, and chill out for a few hours. As Neistat says, "It's the only way to maintain order."

Some Instagram stats have stated that the weekends will provide the most interactions with customers, but it is best for every retailer to run studies of their own. Statigram.com is a free service that breaks down all the analytics of the Instagram feed. Providing the information retailers need to tailor their stream to their fans.

Instagram Pre-Post Checklist

Running a checklist prior to posting on social can be a challenge. After running through the checklist a dozen times the process will become second nature.

Is the image artful? Photos should tell a story in their art and should have a filter. I recommend one feature. Filter, frame, tilt shift, or contrast. Not all of them at once.

Is the image aligned with the store's theme or story? Posting photos of puppies or large breasted women will get a lot of interaction, but not the type of interaction most IBRs want. Stick to the theme of the business.

Is the story appealing to a younger generation? The majority of Instagram users are under 25 and make less than $30,000 a year.

Posting direct or public? Some images are best for the public feed while others are best for a select group. Using Instagram's direct feature allows the retailer to communicate to a specific person or group of people. If the photo is best suited for a smaller group, save the majority of customers by sending it direct.

Strava

The great thing about platforms like Facebook, Twitter, and Instagram is that nearly everyone uses them. For creating connection, getting a name out, and building a large community the platforms work wonderfully. The horrible thing about those platforms is that nearly everyone uses them. It's easy to get lost in Facebook's algorithm or get pushed down the feed on Twitter and Instagram.

All IBRs have one thing in common, their customers are cyclists. If an IBR wants to make a connection to their customers with discussions on cycling there can sometimes be too much noise on Facebook, Twitter, and Instagram. For a retailer to fully understand how their customers are using and enjoying their bike they would have to scroll through pages of updates about their kids, photos of their feet on a beach, and check-ins from their favorite restaurants. While there are far fewer users than the platforms I've already mentioned, Strava provides a clear signal and allows IBRs to watch their customers do the one thing they want them to be doing, riding their bike.

As it states on the Strava website, "Strava lets athletes all over the world experience social fitness—sharing, comparing and competing with each other's personal fitness data via mobile and online apps. Currently focused on the needs of avid cyclists and runners, Strava lets you track your rides and runs via your iPhone, Android or dedicated GPS device to analyze and quantify your performance. Strava makes fitness a social experience, providing motivation and camaraderie even if you're exercising alone."[22] On the surface everyone can see the value of Strava as a tool to track their rides, but the real value for IBRs is the social element of the platform. When people use Strava they are connected to everyone they ride and are measured against everyone who has ever ridden that road or trail before them.

In September of 2013 Lesley-Anne Mallon wrote a blog post for Bicycling in South Africa. The blog was titled, "Addicted To Strava".[23] The words "addicted" and "Strava" seem to be combined in the psyche of cyclists everywhere. A Google search for the phrase "addicted to Strava" brings up over 12,000 results, mostly blog posts from people proclaiming their love to the platform. People have made t-shirts saying "Strava Addict" and "Strava led me to doping." At the start of group rides everywhere you will hear cyclists tell each other, "Strava or it didn't happen." After the ride they quickly reach for their phones to upload their data and see how they performed. It can be argued that no other brand has been more successful at getting people to ride their bike than Strava.

In her blog post Mallon recounted some features of the platform. "Strava is amazing; it's like Facebook for cyclists! Not only can you connect and follow your friends but it also magically picks up who you rode with." Despite having over 3 million users (and growing) Strava is a micro-social platform in that it focuses on a very specific actions, primarily cycling and running. For an IBR, a tool like Strava is just as important to the social strategy as Facebook, Twitter, or Instagram.

As it sits now most retailers sell a bike and begin the hoping game. Where the retailer hopes the customer comes back, hopes they ride the bike, hopes they enjoy it, and hopes that they will connect with their Facebook page. Instead of hoping retailers can use Strava to create a direct connection with cyclists, they could constantly congratulate them on rides well done, introduce them to other riders, and make suggestions on where to ride.

I encourage IBRs to start a Strava Club for their store and after each bike sale teach customers about the platform, how it works, and the benefits of using it. Then have them sign up in store so the customer can be part of the club immediately. Once people have joined the club the retailer can receive a daily digest which details how their customers are using their bikes. This gives the retailer a unique opportunity to make a positive and very specific connection. When a retailer sees that someone has ridden 1000 miles they can congratulate them, make a recommendation to check their tires for wear, ask how the bike is shifting, or suggest that next month they aim for 1500 miles. Every member of the club will also appear on a weekly leaderboard so the retailer can see who is, and isn't riding, and act accordingly. On the club page retailers can host chats on the discussion boards, post their favorite routes, and announce when the next shop ride is.

Tone. The tone on Strava is just as important as it is with any other platform. It needs to represent the IBR well and always follow the two rules of marketing, to be connected and to be helpful. Unlike other platforms Strava does not allow a business to post on behalf of a business, there are only user profiles. Retailers should dedicate people to post on behalf of the store.

Comment on Customer Rides. It Strava's current set-up it is cumbersome for a retailer to comment on someone's ride. The fastest way is to scroll through the feed and comment when appropriate. However this feed will only show one ride at a time, for any cumulative data a retailer must visit each customer page individually. With cumulative data it is easier for the retailer to make suggestions on rides, goals, service, and replacement parts.

Many people on Strava will fall into the Kudos trap (Kudos on Strava are equivalent to a Like on Facebook) where they hit the Kudos button and leave only congratulatory comments. This is great the first time, but every time the retailer says, "Great job!" they lose meaning behind it. Instead I challenge retailers to add value with their comments. Teach customers about a nearby route, how they could improve their sprint, when to ride to get the least amount of headwind, and so on. The more helpful the retailers are, the better the Strava experience will be for the customers and the more they will ride.

Club Page Announcements, Discussion, and Recent Activity. I encourage every retailer to build a club page and have as many customers as possible sign up to that page. This will allow the retailer to see who has ridden, where they have ridden, and when.

The Club Page has two functions of communication, announcements and discussions. Announcements are messages from the club admins while discussions are open to everyone. However, I have found the best feature to be Recent Activity. In this tab you will be able to see everyone following your shop and quickly offer kudos and comments.

Branding Routes and Segments. Retailers can insert their brand by naming specific routes or segments after their store. Done conservatively, over time the area's best segments can carry new monikers. What once was "Highway 9 Hill" could become the "Mike's Bikes Hill".

Strava Pre-Post Checklist

As you use Strava to post your personal rides or comment on behalf of your club, remember that you represent the business at all times on Strava.

Is your comment helpful? Saying congratulations is nice but after a while it can become annoying and lose its meaning. Instead posts should be helpful and well thought out.

Do your comments inspire them to ride again? The more customers ride their bikes the better the IBR business will do. Every post should allude to the next ride.

Is the comment brief? Strava is not the platform for lengthy comments. Short and succinct comments are best. Aim for under 80 characters.

Are posts on the discussion board helpful or engaging? Posting on the discussion boards should be to the benefit of the club or to create discussion. Ask questions, ask for responses on a new idea, and offer solutions.

Links work. Strava currently does not allow direct messaging, tagging, hashtags, or embedding. It does offer links though. While it goes against the rules of proper social engagement, a retailer can post links to other sites where a more customized engagement is possible.

Hashtags

The hashtag, formerly known to anyone in Generation X or older as the pound sign, is a form of metadata tagging. I like to explain it with this analogy; if the internet were a filing cabinet then hashtags are the folders that hold things together. Although hashtags were not invented by the folks at Twitter, they were popularized by them. In August of 2007 Chris Messina (@factoyjoe) posted on Twitter, "How do you feel about using # (pound) for groups. As in #barcamp [msg]? Since this post hashtags have seen mass adoption and can now be used on nearly all major social media platforms. Twitter, Facebook, and Instagram all use hashtags to categorize content.

The most popular hashtag in cycling history popped up in January of 2013 when Oprah Winfrey held a two-part special with Lance Armstrong. In the interview Armstrong admitted to using performance enhancing drugs throughout his career despite having vehemently denying it for over a decade. When users on Twitter combined Armstrong's doping with Oprah Winfrey, the hashtag #doprah was born, and it grew to spawn thousands of tweets. Some examples:

This Lance Armstrong interview would have been better if he and Oprah were riding stationary bikes. #doprah - @BarrettAll

"And I would have gotten away with it too if it weren't for those meddlesome kids!" -lance #doprah - @cjammet

Guys don't do it. This "interview" is just a trap to get men to watch Oprah! #doprah - @burgerboxxx

Lance Armstrong was so upset during his confession that Oprah leaned over and gave him a performance enhancing hug #doprah - @olivercallan

#doprah is a perfect example of the two most powerful elements of a viral hashtag; relevance and humor. Albeit, having those two will not guarantee a viral reaction- it can't hurt either. Here are some great ways to use hashtags in communication.

Own your business' conversation. An IBR should start by searching the hashtag for their business name; #yourbikeshopname - if they haven't done this, odds are good people are already talking about them and they're missing an opportunity to be involved in those conversations.

Don't join the wrong conversation. Sometimes a hashtag can be so common it may already be in use. Not checking for existing names can lead to embarrassing results. There are several bike retailers using #bikebarn. While it is a perfectly logical hashtag to use, there are nearly twenty businesses in the US named Bike Barn and many of them are using the same hashtag.

Create discussion. If retailers want to host a regular Q&A session on a social platform creating a hashtag for it can be an easy way to sort all the incoming questions. For example: #bikebarnquestions. Maybe they want to start a discussion about what people are riding (#mybikeis) or inform people of something they should consider or know more about (#vote4bikelanes).

Have fun. As I mentioned earlier, everyone should have fun with their hashtags- relevance and humor are a retailer's friends.

Need Great Content? RPM It

Millions of experts, authors, bloggers, and journalists have already said it but it is worth repeating. In today's world of online marketing, content is king. People will only respond to social feeds or web content if it is compelling.

One of the most daunting elements of creating any content is deciding what to write about. Many people just can't imagine that anything they have to say is important or relevant enough to have other people read it. Once a retailer does find something to write about the secondary challenge is that the content should be relevant, timely, and useful. If the content was also newsworthy and aligned with current trends it'd be more likely to succeed. To combat these challenges I have developed a system for creating great content that achieves in engagement and relevance. I call the system RPM, or Rip, Pivot, and Move.

Rip. When struggling for content, IBRs may need to borrow some inspiration- and when I say "borrow" I mean "rip it off". Start by searching for something that is currently trending in the world. (I recommend using Google Hot Trends to find out what is most relevant in your community). At the time of writing this Black Friday and Cyber Monday are trending very well. This means that these topics are at the forefront of public consciousness. When retailers can create content that aligns with current trends they are more likely to have their posts shared, liked, and commented on. This is RIPping off the idea.

Pivot. This is where the mainstream idea is recreated for the readers. With something as popular as Black Friday any retailer could quickly jump to reminding people of their Black Friday specials, but that would not be original. Everyone will be doing that. Instead I would write the top ten ways to do Black Friday shopping by bike and within the list feature many of the products sold in the store.

Move. Once a retailer has an idea that will leverage current cultural trends, it's time to MOVE this idea to market and get people on board. This means scheduling posts on social feeds, emailing a links out to customers, taking photos of a fully set-up Black Friday bike and posting it to Instagram.

Using the RPM method to generate content will help retailers ensure that what they are creating has the highest likelihood of reader engagement. To providea head start I have listed out what I feel defines great content, and in each definition I added an idea for a post that any retailer could start writing immediately.

Compelling argument that sparks conversation
Why doping should/should not be allowed in the pro peloton
Why riding is better/not better than running
Why Paleo diets for cyclists are silly/awesome

A unique observation
What streets would look like if 10% of motorists rode bikes.
Why I chose to ride 26/650b/29
A collection of our customers Ironman tattoos

An awesome recipe with photos
Pre-race pasta
Making stroopwafels for the ride
How to brew the world's best post ride beer

A cool DIY project
Rebuilding a classic 1981 Stumpjumper
How to build a custom wheel set
Best cycling concepts on Kickstarter

A helpful tip on anything
The best bike ride you can do in 30 minutes
The best bike locks for under $50
The most aero component for your money

A touching story through photos
15 Instagram photos of my kid learning to ride
A customer's journey on this year's AIDs Ride
Photos of people riding with their dogs

A challenge to take action
Join Club 100 and commit to riding 100 miles every month
Join our commute challenge for Bike to Work Week
Meet us for our group ride this Thursday

A personal struggle and what it has taught you
The hardest ride I've ever done
The worst cycling purchase I've ever made
How cycling helped me lose weight

A funny list
Top ten names for a saddle sore
Funniest requests we've ever gotten
Toughest professional cyclists

An original idea brought to life
How we built the world's lightest bike
How our bike shop grew 400% in one year
Before and after photos of our new service area

Something that evokes an emotional response
Check out this video of my kid riding park
Why American Flyers is better than Breaking Away
Man with no legs completes an Ironman

Something that makes people feel better about themselves
How bike riding makes you a better parent
The money you can save from riding your bike
We all fall down. The story of first time clipless pedals users

Some of these ideas can be a 140 character tweet, some could be posts on Facebook, and others could be a stream of photos on Instagram. Once a retailer chooses the content they'd like to create, the next step is finding the best way to communicate it.

Building a Calendar

If content is king then distribution is queen. Delivering content can be just as important as creating it. The world is a cluttered and noisy place and it can be very difficult to have a message heard if that message is not aligned with greater trends. I encourage all retailers to build a marketing calendar that leverages events both inside and outside the sport of cycling.

Events around the sport of cycling make the most sense. No one would blink an eye if a bike retailer held a Tour de France event or a local trail building day. These events correlate nicely with the business. However, since they are cycling events they are more focused on cyclists and could potentially limit the reach to new customers.

I have put together a calendar of events by month for each retailer to use as a guide to building their marketing and content distribution calendar. I do not believe a retailer should have a campaign for every possible event. Rather choose the events that tie in well with the business ethos.

Specific and/or Recurring Events
Store's anniversary
Owner and employee birthdays
Weekly, monthly, annual rides (fun rides, charity rides, training rides)
Weekly, monthly, annual bike races or triathlons
Local holidays
Concerts
Local sporting events
Alleycats
Events at nearby universities
Farmer's markets
Store sale events
Manufacturer events (demo nights, industry nights)
Strava Challenges

January (start planning in October):
Levi's GranFondo
Tour Down Under
Cyclocross National Championships
National Doprah Day
New Year's Day
National Cut Your Energy Costs Day
Martin Luther King Day
Get to Know Your Customer Day
National Pie Day

Chinese New Year
Diet Resolution Week
Get Organized Month
Back-to-School

February (start planning in November):
Stupor Bowl
National Freedom Day
Groundhog Day
Super Bowl
National Wear Red Day
Lincoln's Birthday
Ash Wednesday
Valentine's Day
President's Day (Washington's Birthday)
Daytona 500
Carnaval
National Chili Day
American Heart Month
National Pancake Week
Black History Month

March (start planning in December):
Milan - San Remo
Gent – Wevelgem
Tour des Flandres
Mellow Johnny's Classic
Bonelli Park
Fontana City
Reaper Madness Downhill & Super D
Cape Epic
Academy Awards
Lent Begins
Daylight Savings Time Starts

Check Your Batteries Day
St. Patrick's Day
March Equinox / First Day of Spring
National Mom & Pop Business Day
National Nutrition Month
March Madness – NCAA Basketball
Birthday of Benito Juarez

April (start planning in January):
Paris – Roubaix
Amstel Gold Race
La Fleche Wallone
Liege – Bastogne – Liege
Tour de Romandie
Redlands Bicycle Classic
Winston – Salem Cycling Classic
Joe Martin Stage Race
Tour of the Gila
Sea Otter Classic
Colorado Springs
Tour of California
April Fool's Day
National Deep Dish Pizza Day
One Day Without Shoes Day
Army Day
National Student Athlete Day
Tax Day
International Zombie Day
National Weed Day (4-20 Day)
Good Friday
Easter
Earth Day
National Jelly Bean Day

Prom
Car Care Month

May (start planning in February):
Giro d'Italia
Collegiate Road National Championships
Elite BMX National Championships
Professional Road & TT National Championships
Mountain Creek Spring Classic
Plattekill Gravity Open
Loyalty Day
May Day
Kentucky Derby
Cinco de Mayo
National Nurses Day
National Teacher Day
No Diet Day
Eat What You Want Day
Mother's Day
National Bike to Work Day
Armed Forces Day
Harvey Milk Day
Indy 500
Memorial Day
National Pet Week
National Bike Month
National Photo Month
National Physical Fitness & Sports Month

June (start planning in March):
Criterium du Dauphine
Tour de Suisse
Philadelphia Cycling Classic
North Star Grand Prix

Colorado Springs – US Cup Pro Series
Missoula XC
Amateur BMX National Championships
24-Hour MTB National Championships
Chile Challenge
California Golden State
Windham US National MTB Race
Missoula XC
SF to LA AIDS Ride
Tweed Cycling Day
National Running Day
D-Day
National Donut Day
Best Friends Day
Flag Day
Father's Day
June Solstice / First Day of Summer
Wimbledon
Let it Go Day
Graduation
National Safety Month
National Soul Food Month
NBA Finals

July (start planning in April):
Tour de France
Cascade Cycling Classic
Marathon MTB National Championships
Cross-Country MTB National Championship
Professional Criterium National Championships
Snowshoe Mountain Pro GRT
Subaru Cup
Specialized Catamount Classic
Leadville 100

North American Cycle Courier Championships

Major Taylor Day

RAGBRAI

Canada Day

World UFO Day

Independence Day

National BBQ Day

National Nude Day

Nelson Mandela Day

National Hot Dog Day/Month

National Ice Cream Day/Month

National All or Nothing Day

August (start planning in May):

Vuelta a Espana

Tour de Park City

Gravity MTB National Championships

Elite Track National Championships

Eurobike

Girlfriend's Day

International Beer Day

Sister's Day

National Underwear Day

National Garage Sale Day

National Relaxation Day

Men's Grooming Day

National Thrift Shop Day

Senior Citizen's Day

Back-to-School

Shark Week

National Scrabble Week

Weird Contest Week

September (start planning in June):
UCI World Championships
Thompson Bucks Cunty Classic
Collegiate Track National Championships
Mammoth Kamikaze Bike Games
Interbike
Labor Day
NFL Regular Season Begins
Be Late For Something Day
National Grandparents Day
Patriot Day
Mexican Independence Day
9/11 Remembrance Day
LGBT Center Awareness Day
National POW/MIA Recognition Day
National HIV/AIDS Awareness Day
Wife Appreciation Day
Family Day
September Equinox / First Day of Fall
Rosh Hashanah
National Good Neighbor Day
National Clean Hands Week
National Coupon Month
National Skin Care Awareness Month
National Waffle Week
Oktoberfest

October (start planning in July):
Tour of Beijing
Collegiate MTB National Championships
Bike Messenger Appreciation Day (10-9 Day)
Yom Kippur
Chinese National Day
Eid-Al-Adha

National Men Make Dinner Day
Columbus Day
Canadian Thanksgiving
Boss's Day
Wear Something Gaudy Day
Smart is Cool Day
National Cat Day
Halloween
AIDS Awareness Month
Mental Illness Awareness Week
National Breast Cancer Awareness Month
World Series

November (start planning in August):
Cranksgiving
El Dia de los Muertos (Day of the Dead)
All Saint's Day
World Vegan Day
Daylight Savings Time Ends
Election Day
Kristallnacht
Veterans Day
Loosen Up, Lighten Up Day
National Day of Play
World Hello Day
Thanksgiving Day
Black Friday
Small Business Saturday
Movember
National Family Week
National Hunger & Homeless Awareness Week
Pursuit of Happiness Week
American Indian Heritage Month

December (start planning in September):

Cyber Monday

Rosa Parks Day

Pearl Harbor Remembrance Day

Nobel Prize Day

Wright Brothers Day

First Day of Hanukkah

December Solstice / First Day of Winter

Festivus

Christmas Eve

Boxing Day

Tolerance Week

Kwanzaa

Christmas Day

New Year's Eve

When building a calendar or content around these events tone is very important. Retailers have ruined their relationship with communities of people because they poorly judged how people would respond to their tone. Here is an example:

Poor Tone: "Come in for our Veteran's Day Sale! All bikes 10% and a free helmet with bike purchase!" This is poor tone because Veteran's Day is not traditionally thought of as a celebratory holiday. It is not a time to get out and grab great deals. It is a day of remembrance and mourning. Instead:

Good tone: "We want to thank all the veterans who have served and given their lives for our country. To them and their families, we thank you." Not every event is about selling, some events are about connecting with the people who have a relationship with the business.

Chapter 7
Vansevenant Checklist

Remember the two rules of marketing. 1) Maintain positive connection to your customers and 2) Be extremely helpful. How are you currently doing these two things?

Think of some examples of how you can spend your time and money on social. The four areas of focus are gratitude, customer service, contextual conversation, and promotion.

Be sure to run through your pre-post checklists

Facebook:
Is the text too long?
Is it provocative, entertaining, or surprising?
Is the photo striking and high quality?
Is the logo or product visible?
Is the call to action in the right place?
Is this interesting in any way, to anyone?
Are you asking too much of the person who is consuming the content?

Twitter:
Is it to the point?
Is the hashtag unique and memorable?
Is the image attached high quality?
Does the voice sound authentic?

Instagram:
Is the image artful?
Is the image aligned with my theme or story?
Is the story appealing to a younger generation?

Strava:
Is your comment helpful?
Do your comments inspire them to ride again?

Is your comment brief?
Are posts on the discussion board helpful or engaging?

Open up Google Trends and find three ideas you can RPM (Rip, Pivot, Move) for your business.

Build a content and marketing calendar. Start planning at least 90 days prior to the event

8

Looking Forward

"All businesses need to be young forever. If your customer base ages with you, you're Woolworth's."
- Jeff Bezos, CEO of Amazon

It's no secret; the sport of cycling is dominated by white people. In 2009 Caucasians were 75% of all bicycle trips in the US .[1] From a glance at most cycling communities it would be safe to assume that cycling is also dominated by men. Younger generations, women, and minorities have all taken a backseat in the sport of cycling and bike retail has reflected it. Nearly every IBR in the North America does not represent women's and men's categories equally and in my experience, images and advertising around the sport are predominantly white and male.

The demographics of the US are changing, or already have changed and the majority customer for many IBRs will no longer be the majority in the marketplace. There are already more women than men in the US[2] and for people born after 2008, Caucasians are no longer the majority.[3] If a bike retailer is underserving women they are not reaching 50% or more of their potential customers. If they are also underserving races that are not white, they have cut their customer base in half again. If their customer base is also 30 years or older, they can cut their potential market in half one more time. As bike retailers drive forward an enormous factor in their growth is understanding and engaging with the customers they have underserved, starting with largest and most misunderstood group in history; Millennials.

Millennials

When a Millennial, or member of Generation Y, was born is up for some debate depending on who is speaking or which blog they're posting to. Years range as early as 1979 and as late as 2005. To make it simple I will define a Millennial as someone who was born between the early 1980s and the early 2000s. Millennials are known for their prolific spending habits, a non-stop connection to their devices, and complete awareness of brands in their lives. Millennials in the US are radically diverse compared to previous generations.[4] In the United States 22% percent of people under the age of fifteen are Hispanic, 14% African American, and 6% are Asian.[5] Millennials who are now entering or leaving university will have the largest amount personal debt compared to any other generation[6] but at the same time they will have the highest education rate in human history.[7] With a weak economy this means Millennials will be entering a flooded workforce where many of them will be underemployed or even unemployed.

According to Elliot Gluskin of the Gluskin Townley Group, there are approximately 43 million Millennials who are 18 years or older with another 57 million who will reach adulthood in the next eight to ten years.[8] How does this all affect a bike retailer? If the 78 million Baby Boomers brought cycling's greatest years in the early 70s, imagine what the 100 million Millennials will do in 2020-2022 when they can't afford to make a car payment. Hence, Millennials will be riding bikes more than any other living generation. According to a 2013 report by the US Public Interest Research Group (PIRG), "The average person ages 16-34 drove 23% less in 2009 than in 2001, the sharpest reduction for any age group."[9]

However, connecting with a Millennial and convincing them that a local IBR is the best place to buy a bike are two completely different stories. A Millennial is known for jumping quickly from brand to brand, and for many marketers having a Millennial remain loyal to one brand for 6-8 months is considered a success. A Millennial is also connected in a way that previous generations cannot even fathom. Their ability to manage and consume multiple screens of content mean they will be the most informed buyer and come into a store with a deep knowledge and understanding of the product they are purchasing. That is if they even bother walking into a brick and mortar store. Millennials live in digital worlds as much or more than their physical worlds. Their comfort, trust, and understanding with online retailers are as good as or greater than their relationship with any brick and mortar.

To engage Millennials IBRs will have to embrace their style of communication by providing them with resourceful, helpful, and easily accessible content that improves their lives. For retailers who are hoping to win the Millennial market they should focus on connection, customization, and cost.

A personal connection. Where Baby Boomers and Generation X point to devices as a loss of human connection, Millennials see their device as their strongest form of connection. They feel that through their phone or tablet they are connected to all their friends, family, coworkers, and role models at the same time. They feel this channel of connection is a two way street and they expect the businesses they buy from to connect with them on a personal level, in the eyes of a Millennial a personal connection is the least a business can do to earn their money.

They want it built for them. In a world where everyone has equal access to everything, the most unique are the most admired. Nike, Adidas, Apple, and a slew of other apparel and technology brands have taken this idea to every extreme by adding customization features to nearly every product they offer. If I want an all-white pair of Nikes with my name on them, no problem and in the same manner Millennials do not want to ride just any bike, they want ride "their bike". The bike that has been designed, built, assembled, and customized perfectly for them. Their purchases are an extension of their identity. A bike retailer can do this by focusing on bike fitting, customizable products, and a menu of services that allow the customer to tailor their purchase to their wants or needs.

They spend wisely. Remember that this is the generation with the most debt in a weak economy combined with the highest education, so they manage their money carefully. While they understand that with more money comes more quality they will not stand for two retailers offering the same product for two different prices.

They are loyal. Sort of. Millennials see brand loyalty very differently than the generations before them. They are devoted and very loyal to the brands and businesses they have grown up with. At the same time they are very open to exploring new options. While they love one bike retailer and may even refer to it as their "home shop" they will not blink an eye at purchasing from another store if they are offering something their home shop is not. An IBR has more success battling this with a hyper focus on their niche rather trying to carry one of everything.

They want to support a cause. Purchase a pair of Toms shoes and they will donate a pair of shoes to a child in need. Warby Parker does the same for eyewear and Lululemon donates to charities combating abuse. When a Millennial purchases from a business it should also mean that something changes for the better in the community or the world. While charities are never meant to be bragged about, politely letting people know that supporting the IBR business supports a cause can be the influence a Millennial needs to commit.

Avoid the hard sell. For Millennials, making a purchase isn't as cut and dried as when a Baby Boomer bought a bike. Millennials understand when they are working with a retailer versus a manufacturer and they can tell when a retailer offers nothing to increase the value of the sale. From a Millennial's point of view, there are unlimited choices and no reason to have qualms about purchasing through another channel. They can purchase the bike from the local IBR, from the bike shop across town, or from the website based in another country. They can buy the bike as a whole unit or buy it in pieces. To a Millennial the hard sell comes off as desperation and stinks of a hidden agenda. At the very least a hard sell will send them back to research mode.

For any business that wants to be around for years to come, selling to Millennials is not a choice, it is a must. Generations come and generations go. The next decades will see the passing of many Baby Boomers, Generation X will become less and less active, and Millennials will comprise the entirety of the customer base. IBRs can't avoid them or wait it out. The time to start engaging Millennials is now.

Women

Across the country women are still earning approximately 80 cents to the dollar when compared to men who have a similar education and career.[10] However, in many major cities like New York, Sacramento, San Diego, Atlanta, Miami, Los Angeles, and Phoenix, women are out-earning men by as much as 19%.[11] Women also dominate higher education at most colleges and universities across the US and Canada with 60% of students being female and those women are earning 149 degrees for every 100 earned by men.[12] The most powerful statistic for a retailer is to know that women control the 73% of active and passive income of their households.[13] Women hold the keys to nearly all the spending and anyone working on the retail floor can account for the hundreds of men who were shopping for a bike but first had to "get permission" from their wives.

While many in the bicycle industry accept these statistics they are quick to say that women just are not interested in cycling. They could not be more wrong. In a report by the League of American Bicyclists, 60% of bicycle owners age 17 to 28 years old are women, 56% more women commuted by bike in 2011 than in 2007, and cycling outranked yoga for total female participation.[14] The Gluskin Townley Group added fuel to the fire with their report showing a sharp change in who was riding their bike. They said, "male bicycle riding participants declining from 55% in 2011 to 51% in 2012, while female participants increased from 45% in

2011 to 49% in 2012."[15] If any bike retailers believe women are not interested in cycling then it is more likely that women just aren't interested in shopping with that particular store.

Nearly every cycling brand has recognized that women are a key to future growth with a wide range of products designed for her and backed with marketing aimed to connect with her. Yet many IBRs have been slow to accept women's cycling in their business stating that past years sales do not warrant greater investment in the current year. This is a problem that does nothing but stagnate growth. In order to grow the women's cycling community we have to invest in it. This means products and services tailored to women with plenty of space dedicated in the store.

For many women, the shopping experience at a local bike retailer will gravitate to one word; intimidating. David Fiedler is the editor for the bicycling pages at About.com, in an article titled 'How to Work With a Bike Shop', Fielder wrote, "Bike shops can be the best place in the world for cyclists. It's somewhere to pass the hours happily talking with the staff about this new bike or that, or a magical spot to bring your broken-down baby so that some wizard at the work stand can make it whole again. Or they can be unpleasant and intimidating, filled with expensive, space-age gear with astronomical price tags and employees who disdain their customers."[16]

The latter sentence describing an "unpleasant and intimidating" bike retailer is a sentiment felt by many first time cyclists, especially women. The intimidation level of many IBRs is difficult to compare. Some riders have used the analogy of "a manly-man shopping for lingerie" or "non-comic fans shopping for comics". In my experience it doesn't seem to matter what the environment is or what products they are stocking- though having some focus on both of those can help. An intimidating store revolves around one thing; the people working there. As bike retailers hope to move the industry forward it will be paramount that they tackle the intimidation factor head on.

On her blog, Mastering The Uphill Shift, Anna Doorenbos had this to say about bike shops, "They [bike shops] seem more exclusive than regular stores, where you are only welcome with open arms if you speak the secret bike language. Someone less prone to intimidation than me would have no problem walking into a bike shop cold turkey and walk out with what they needed. Not me. I really have to work up courage to walk into a shop! It can only take one rude or condescending sales person to make the trip miserable. In addition, the people who work at bike shops are often very passionate about what they do (because with the kind of money they (don't) make, they're the only ones who will work there). And sometimes that zeal can be seen as condescension, or it can make it hard to relate to a person who is not an expert like them. In general, I think those in bike shops are awesome people, but it doesn't always seem that way at first glance."[17]

To understand better, it is important that to determine whether or not the intimidation factor within a bike retailer is something that we should worry about. Here are common signs that an IBR is intimidating.

She brings an expert along. Many customers come into a store with their "expert" in tow. The expert could be a spouse, friend, or coworker but no matter the relationship they always know more about cycling than the person who is looking for a new bike. The expert is not there to help them figure out which bike to buy, the expert is there to protect the buyer from getting sold products they do not need. If the person working on the retail floor wasn't so aggressive in their sales approach the store wouldn't have the reputation that it is beneficial to have an expert in tow.

She doesn't want help. Customers walk in the store and avoid any type of communication with the staff. No matter the approach, they just don't want to talk. This can stem from a fear of being belittled, not respected, or an oncoming price negotiation.

She wants to do more research. This is a classic problem. Those working on the retail floor will chat with a customer for 30-40 minutes and then the customer leaves with nothing but a business card and a catalog. Why did this happen? It happens when staff inundates the customer with his vast knowledge of construction methods, componentry spec, wheel sizes, and aerodynamic hypotheses. This overload of information can send the customer spiraling into a world of confusion and uncertainty.

They may have come into the store with an idea of what they were looking for, but after talking to someone they weren't sure, now they need to head back home to do some more research.

She doesn't even bother. The worst is when a store has established itself as such an intimidating shop that no one even visits the store. This is one reason it would be beneficial to record new customers coming in. If new customer acquisition is shrinking dramatically it may be a sign that potential customers are being scared off.

While these reasons are not absolute proof of an intimidating environment, they can be a sign of bad things to come.

Tribe Building

Seth Godin is an author, entrepreneur, and marketer. In 2008 Godin published Tribes: We Need You to Lead Us.[18] In the book Godin teaches us that through history, big world-changing actions can be lumped into three very big ideas.

The first idea was that anyone could change the world by building a factory. Godin argued that if one can combine productive people with a simple-to-follow set of instructions then they could change the world with their ability to produce. If we traveled back in time to 20th century Chicago we would see this idea demonstrated to its fullest. In the 1890s the US was the world leader in bicycle manufacturing and the epicenter of production was Chicago, Illinois. Led by Schwinn, Chicago was home to over thirty factories turning out thousands of bikes every day. The idea of factory work was so big that the US grew to over a million bicycles built every year before the turn of the 20th century. Long before Henry Ford built his iconic assembly line to produce the Model-T, Schwinn was proving the concept.

Godin's second idea had to do with advertising, television, media, and promotion. The idea was if someone talked about their idea enough and pushed it on people, it could also change the world. If a bike retailer wanted to sell more bikes in the 1980s the formula was pretty simple; buy ad space. If they bought prime time print, radio, and television ads in their city they were guaranteed to reach a very large portion of the market. If they bought ads on multiple channels and the results were even better.

The third idea is for a post internet world, where resources are limited and getting a majority of market attention through traditional media is so expensive most IBRs cannot afford it. This is the idea of connecting like-minded people and leading them to a place they want to go. This is building and leading a store's community. The internet means factories and traditional media are no longer important. Now a bike retailer can connect 100, 500, or 5000 people who want make a change or participate in something new and can then show them a path. Any IBR can lead their community.

As manufacturers battle to sell high quantities at low prices, as more and more brands move online and sell directly to customers, the one stronghold retailers will maintain is the attention and leadership of their community, or as Godin would put it, "their tribe".

Tribe building involves many elements. It is a balance of having a spectacular idea, a unique and differentiated service, and a way of speaking to the tribe that no one else can replicate or wants to replicate. One of the most noticeably recognized tribes in the world of cycling are bike messengers. While bike messengers are often seen as reckless and dangerous to everyone around them, many people don't recognize the enormous cultural contribution that bike messengers have made. In his book, Brand Hijack: Marketing Without Marketing, Alex Wipperfurth claimed that bike messengers were the catalyst for meteoric sales of Pabst Blue Ribbon.[19] While other beers were sponsoring the Super Bowl Halftime Show, PBR was writing checks to bike messengers as sponsorship for bike polo events, alleycats, and anything else they could think of. By investing in the tribe of bike messengers PBR saw a growth of 134 percent in Chicago and for the first time in their history started to top the charts in Portland and San Francisco, cities known for their beer snobbery.[20]

Throughout the past decade the allure of bike messenger culture has been the focus for many brands, but it is not an easy nut to crack. Bike messengers are notoriously fickle, anti-

197

corporate, anti-brand, and can spot a phony trying to pander to them from 20 blocks away. Not everyone can be as successful as PBR was. When PUMA wanted bike messengers to ride in their shoes, or when Bern wanted messengers to wear helmets, or if when a Hollywood action film about messengers needed a level of authenticity... they all ended up talking to someone who leads the tribe of bike messengers. They ended up talking to Squid.

Kevin "Squid" Bolger has been a bike messenger since 1992, is president of the New York Bike Messenger Association, and through his career has established himself as an authority figure in the tribe of New York bike messengers. If any brand wanted to sell something to a group of messengers they needed to first establish themselves as a trustworthy, next they had to prove that they were vested in the growth or betterment of the messenger community, and to do that they had to start by convincing Squid.

Squid worked with PUMA in the 2004 to form Team PUMA, a 5-member race team comprised of only bike messengers. In a press release for the team PUMA North America Marketing Director, Barney Waters said, "Bike messengers embody the individuality, style and athleticism that is synonymous with our brand." Wasting no time to reveal the true purpose of this partnership, Waters makes it clear that he wants messengers and anyone who idolizes messengers to see PUMA as the brand for them. He goes on to say "For them, like us, sport is a way of life; it doesn't just end when the day is over, it is part of who they are and how they define themselves. Bike messengers are connected to the city in ways that no other group could be. Through their community, they have shaped modern culture and have become part of the urban landscape."[21]

While Squid's relationship with PUMA didn't stand the test of time, his relationship with Bern helmets has. Squid started wearing Bern helmets in 2005 and recently worked with them to create a video discussing helmets in messenger culture. Squid is considered part of the Bern Urban team, his image is used in full page ads, and he even has his own page on the brand's website. In his bio the people at Bern wrote, "You could say Squid Bolger is responsible for Bern being a bike brand."[22] Implying that without Squid's buy-in they may not have ever sold helmets to cyclists.

In 2012 Joseph Gordon-Levitt played a bike messenger in the movie Premium Rush.[23] When filming the producers and directors wanted an authentic feel to the movie and that meant buy-in from New York messengers was important. To do this Director David Koepp went on a search to find the right people to advise him and quickly found Squid. An article in the New York Post described the meeting between Koepp and Squid. "He [Koepp] started asking around at bike shops and courier companies. It was inevitable that fingers would point to Bolger, a 20-year veteran who's something of a legend among messengers in New York City."[24] Through the meeting Koepp hired Squid as a technical consultant on the film and he even makes a cameo in the films opening scenes. (Gordon-Levitt's character wears a Bern helmet in the film as well; think Squid had something to do with that? I do.)

It is apparent that Squid leads his tribe, but do IBRs lead their tribe? When a brand wants to sell a product to cyclists in a given area, do they absolutely need the local IBR to do it? Or are they confident they can sell it with or without them? When a company wants to understand how to develop a product for riders, who do they call? Do they call bike retailer, or do they just reach out to the riders and leave the retailer out of the loop? In a modern economy the strongest currency is the size of the community and the platform in which retailers speak to them. Bike retailers that lead their tribe, not just sell to them, will be absolutely essential going forward. If retailers control the tribe of cyclists around them, they hold all the cards. Every manufacturer, vendor, and brand will bend to their wishes.

How Running Stores Lead Tribes

A New York Times article from September of 2013 titled The Finish Line Starts Here interviewed owners of specialty running stores in New York.[25] One of those interviews was with Lee Silverman, owner of JackRabbit Sports, the largest independently owned running store in New York. Silverman said, "Coming into a good running store and getting the right gear is definitely part of the experience we offer, but mostly, runners want to get out and run. We want to be part of that experience too." To be part of that experience, JackRabbit Sports coordinates eight free weekly group runs, for people of all fitness levels. Pacers include JackRabbit staff members, members of running teams and sometimes elite competitors.

Bike retailers could learn from running stores like JackRabbit. IBRs can often get lost in the minutiae of selling a bike and forget about helping the customer truly experience the sport of cycling. Bike retailers that dedicate themselves to growing their community and improving their service offerings will be the most suited for the next decade of change.

As the bike industry is slower to move their catalog of goods online, the entire floor of a running store is filled with items that can be purchased from the manufacturer websites- and in many cases it can be found cheaper. In many ways, how a running store is operated today is a blueprint for how bike retailers will have to operate in the future. So how do running stores stay afloat when everything they sell can be purchased from a phone?

When I bring this up to IBR owners and managers, a popular response is that running stores can survive because there are more people running than cycling. They believe the customer base of runners is so much larger that they can work on massive volume. This is incorrect. Running participation in the US is nearly identical to cycling. In a 2013 study done by the National Sporting Goods Association the number of people participating in cycling or running activities was very similar, with 39.3 million people cycling and 40 million people running. The NSGA classifies participants as those who ride or run at least six times during a calendar year. The NSGA then takes the total number of participants and breaks it up into three categories: frequent, occasional, and infrequent.[26]

Total participants (in millions):
39.3 cycling, 40.03 running

Frequent, more than 110 days per year:
5.35 cycling, 9.22 running

Occasional, 25-109 days per year:
18.55 cycling, 18.56 running

Infrequent, 6-24 days per year:
15.41 cycling, 12.23 running

While the number of runners and number of cyclists may be similar, there is one reason many bike retailers will call out when they are compared to a thriving running stores. There just are not as many running retailers as bike retailers and therefore the running stores command a larger portion of the market. In this instance, they are correct.

According to Leisure Trends Group there are more than 1038 specialty running stores in the US, compared to just over 4000 independent bike retailers. Though it should be noted that Leisure Trend's numbers only reflect specialty stores, they do not include everyone who is selling running shoes. Those 1038 stores represent approximately 22% percent of all running shoes sold, the remaining 78% is split amongst online retailers, general sporting goods stores, and discount stores. In a similar fashion 74% of bicycles sold in the US are sold by department stores and discount stores. [27]

We've discussed the predicted decline of bike retailers going forward in earlier chapters. Since the number of bikes being sold in the market has been surprisingly stable for more than 10 years, when it comes to selling bikes the pie hasn't gotten bigger, retailers have just started to take a larger slice. For bike retailers, surviving the next 10 years will depend on two things, both of which running stores do very well; leading the tribe and offering a very unique service.

Gary Muhrcke is the owner of Super Runners Shops in Manhattan and in Huntington, on Long Island. He was the very first winner of the New York City Marathon in 1970 and like many bike retailers, turned his passion into a business. In a New York Times article from 2008 titled, Competition Gaining on Running Gear Stores, Muhrcke said personal service was the key to his longevity. "I can't see the shape of a person's foot over the phone," he said. "I can't do gait analysis over the phone. I can't look at a person's body structure or size whether they're bowlegged over the internet." He added, "The basic reason why we're still here- we're needed."[28]

Many bike retailers could sympathize with Muhrcke and many have even said nearly the exact same thing about their business. In order to truly help someone with their bicycle, it has to be done face to face. While this is true, the change in consumerism has proven it is only true for the services provided not the products sold.

Wiggle is a UK-based online retailer that sells everything needed to become a cyclist. The website serves customers worldwide, is translated into ten different languages, operates with fifteen different currencies, and in 2013 had sales north of £140 million ($225 million). Companies like Wiggle have made the brick and mortar nightmare come true. A customer no longer needs a bike shop to buy a bike, or a helmet, jersey, or a pair of cycling shoes. All of those purchases can be done from the comfort of a couch and the buyer will likely save a good amount of money in the process. With a company like Wiggle around, many people are beginning to believe the only thing someone would need an IBR for is to build and repair that bike.

Leading the tribe is the best way brick and mortar retailers can combat giants like Wiggle. Some of the best ways to lead a tribe include promoting internal competition, creating a low barrier to entry, creating a sense of positive sacrifice, and being enthusiastically supportive. All of which running stores do very, very well. I will elaborate:

Promoting internal competition. When compared, competitive cycling could learn quite a bit from competitive running. Nearly every bike race in the US is generally a small venue. At even some of the country's largest bike races it's still pretty easy to find a place to stand near the finish line. In competitive cycling nearly everyone racing is male and the demographics report from USA Cycling confirms it. USA Cycling has over 70,000 members (of which only 13% are female).[29] The number of participants at just Boston Marathon is nearly half of all bike licensed bike racers combined; 26,839 participants (43% were women).[30] Competitive running events are a dominant force in the US and dwarf competitive cycling in every way.

If the sport of competitive cycling is going to ever grow to their numbers to match competitive running it would be good to learn one lesson; the majority of competitive runners are not competing against someone else- they are competing against themselves. At the front of a running race there is a very small handful of runners who have a chance at winning, everyone else is out to set a PR, or personal record. Anyone who hangs out after the finish of any running event will see a showing of support so massive they might be tempted to think that everyone who ran the race also won the race. That's because, in a way, they did.

In bike racing there is no way to measure performance from one event to another except to compare results against other people. The structure of running events is built around measuring individual pace. Measuring pace as it compares to the winner is something that is rarely talked about.

IBRs will have more success building a community of competitive cyclists if they helped cyclists measure repeated performances against themselves. Placing less focus on the winner and more focus on how people did compared to their last effort. I would encourage bike retailers to sponsor or host timed events, or time trials. A weekly 20k time trial is perfectly suited to have massive adoption across all demographics. Another way is to use a software program like Strava which allows the retailer to see everyone who recorded a PR on any given ride- assuming they have done the ride before. Breaking down the categories cyclists can compete in will also help. Splitting groups by gender, then age, and then even by type of bike they are using. Anything the IBR can do that allows someone to compete against themself is going to prove more fruitful toward building the tribe of cyclists

Create a low barrier to entry. In the book Switch: How to Change Things When Change is Hard, authors Chip Heath and Dan Heath discuss the idea of shaping the path.[31] This is where someone will focus on reducing any barriers that might keep someone else from participating in an event, joining a club, or heading out for a run.

When building a cycling community how do bike retailers shape the path for their riders and guide them to joining? They can start by promoting all the positive, path clearing things that their events are: free of charge, a great place to socialize, a wonderful way to experience the roads, led by expert technicians, easy parking, low-traffic routes, a no-drop ride, free water, held after work, and so on.

Create a sense of positive sacrifice. When it comes to moving people to achieve it can never hurt to add an element of sacrifice to the event. People who attend a group ride that starts at 6:30am have sacrificed their sleep. People who ride no matter the weather have sacrificed their comfort. As cycling gets more difficult it borders on the definition of "epic". A bike retailer should grab hold of these epic moments and promote them proudly. This is creating a sense of positive sacrifice.

Positive sacrifice breeds sharing. Waking up on a freezing morning is something cyclists will tell other people about. It's something to brag about. A photo of someone pushing their limits until they collapse is a photo they are proud to share. In an IBR's tribe it can never hurt to have a sense of positive sacrifice. I would encourage retailers to look into ways to create positive sacrifice. Can they host an early morning ride? Can they challenge people to a summit local climb? Can they inspire people to push themselves to a point of discomfort?

Immensely enthusiastic support. It is very easy for cyclists to fall into the trap of a highly competitive, winner takes the glory, mentality. In a great cycling tribe the retailer is sure to avoid lavish attention to the fastest or strongest, instead focusing attention on the achievement of either every individual or the group as a whole. Awarding the most improved, or the greatest sacrifice, or the person who showed the most courage will make the tribe truly inclusive.

Chapter 8
Vansevenant Checklist

How can you create a personal connection with Millennials, as they are the next generation of buyers?

Which services can be made more customizable?

How can you help your customers spend wisely?

What causes do you support and how are you promoting them as a differentiator in your business model?

Talk to your staff and discuss why hard selling is seen as a negative.

Are there signs that your store may be intimidating to women? If so, what are they?

How can your business better embrace women?

How do you lead and command your tribe?

How do you promote internal competition among your customers?

What are the barriers to entry to be a customer of yours? How can we lower these barriers?

Joining your tribe of cyclists means having a sense of positive sacrifice, how are you cultivating this?

What are the best examples you have of providing enthusiastic support to your tribe?

Conclusion

"Change, now it's time for change.
Nothing stays the same. Now it's time for change."
- Motley Crue

In the beginning of the book I quoted Thomas Edison having said, "Genius is one percent inspiration, ninety-nine percent perspiration." Anyone can have an idea. Ideas, in the relative scheme of things, are easy. Putting an idea into place on the other hand is very difficult. As you're about to put the book down I want to remind you that the biggest chunk of work is still to come and it won't be easy, retail is a hard business, but hopefully with the ideas in this book you feel more capable to take some action.

Accomplishing a task and putting a new idea, service, or product out into the world is no small feat. Many people believe that change requires risk, and they're correct. Change requires a willingness to stick your neck out, a willingness to fail, and a willingness to stand up against the people who disagree with the change. All change is going to be challenged and is never guaranteed for success.

Everyone wants to make a change of some sort, yet so few do. Tasks like building a new service menu or changing an opening procedure may seem simple on the surface, but when it comes time to implement many get stuck in a rut. This happens when owners and managers do not effectively plan the changes they want to make. Without a proper plan in place unexpected hurdles are reasons to stop and reasons why "it will never work".

To conclude this book I want to present the questions retailers should ask themselves before attempting to make a change in the business. These questions come from my years of experience watching many, many ideas fail. After each failure I went back and asked myself, "What should I have considered at the beginning to avoid this failure at the end?" By building a proper structure of questions in the beginning, I found that many unexpected barriers became minor tasks to solve. On to the questions:

1. Does this change align with your business ethos? Not all changes are meant for you, and that's ok. The changes you make should align with your businesses' vision and goals. I worked with a retailer in California that wanted to increase traffic on its social platforms and website. After some quick research they found that they received the highest rate of click-through and engagement when they posted photos of attractive women riding bikes; often while wearing revealing clothing. Now while this was one way to create response and engagement, over time it eroded their brand and how they were perceived by the community. Make sure the changes you want to make are aligned with your goals.

2. Is the change about you? Remodeling a service area, installing a new pricing structure, revising the discounting policy, and launching marketing campaigns are all within the ability of your business. If you are looking to change the pricing structure from your vendors or increase the perception of cyclists in the city, this may require other businesses to change. The latter is far more complicated than the former. If the change is not about you, it does not mean it is impossible. It may just be more difficult.

3. Is it crucial to the success of the business, or would it be just nice to have? Some changes happen because of dire circumstances. Perhaps you're losing money or nearby competition is drawing your customers away. It is important to define the changes you'd like to make and their overall importance to the business. This will allow you to focus on what needs to be done rather than what would be fun to do.

4. Has there been demand for this change? If so, when, where, and by whom? Your customers, vendors, and business partners can often see your next steps better than you. They can play the role of impartial third eye on the business and help you point out your weaknesses. It's important to constantly ask the people we serve and work with how we can become better. If people tell you that is difficult to bring a bike through your front door, then you may need to install a sliding door. If people tell you that your technician is intimidating then perhaps you need to have a word with him. If customers tell you that your repair times are too long perhaps you need to hire more staff to handle the volume of work. Constantly gauging and recording demand will bring more clarity to the changes you need to make.

5. How does this change benefit your customers? Some changes improve processes so customers get faster service. Some changes create a better shopping experience. Other changes will give them a better experience on the bike. Every change should be made with the most important person in mind; your customer.

6. How will you make a profit from this? Ultimately every change you make comes down to a profit and loss analysis. Will the change bring enough money to the business to justify the cost? Sometimes it will be easy to see how you will profit. For example, bringing in a new line of mountain bikes can attract a different customer and open up a new segment of sales. Other times seeing how you will profit can be more difficult, buying new uniforms for your staff may not have a direct tie to the cash till but perhaps your customers will be less intimidated when your staff look more professional.

If you can present a thorough analysis on costs versus profit you're likely to inspire your team and yourself to act on the change.

7. Can the change be leveraged in multiple ways? Sponsoring a second or third cycling club can garner more clout in the community and perhaps drive some traffic through the door, therefore it may be a worthwhile change for the bike shop to make. Though is that its only benefit? What if the new cycling clubs were required to lead and host your shop rides as well, freeing up staff to either stay at home or enjoy the ride for themselves? Finding multiple ways to leverage the change will give you more reasons to execute and help bring people on board with your idea.

8. Can you enlist resources from outside your circle to get this done? You and your staff can do all the work to make the change, but do you have to? If you've seen it as a challenge in your business, odds are good that someone else has as well. How did they solve it and can you borrow their solution? Perhaps your vendors have helped other bike shops with this same problem. Perhaps the hiking store across town built the solution and is willing to sell or lease it to you? Consider all your options for solving the problem before marching out on your own.

9. How much will this cost to do? It's an obvious question to have answered, especially if you have to get buy-in from an owner or financier. Knowing the base costs is good, but to take it a step further have these questions answered as well: Has it been budgeted? Is there a cheaper way to achieve the same result? Will this expense be a one-time expense or recurring? If it is recurring, how often will it be, weekly, monthly or annually?

It is also important to consider more than just the costs of parts or supplies. How many man hours will be used? Will you need to hire a consultant or contractor? Will you have to hire builders, plumbers, or electricians? Considering all costs will help you foresee many of the barriers that often stop other people from making the change.

10. What will it cost if you do not make this change? Answering this question is best when it is analytical, not anecdotal. The answer will often sound like this, "If we do not make this change we stand to lose $3500 each month to our competitor." Have some precise data to support your claim. Tying your change to a dollar amount lost is a powerful way to get people on board with the idea.

11. Are you achieving this change already? Perhaps you want to double sales in your business over the next year. Looking through your records, is there a time of year when you're already meeting the sales goal you want to hit? Even if it is for just one day, you can learn quite a bit. What type of staffing did you have? How did you handle the influx of bikes coming in and out? Who rose to occasion and handled the work with poise? By pointing to the times when you already succeed the desired goal, you can lay a good amount of the groundwork to making the change more often.

12. How will you inspire and empower your staff to make this change? A great idea is only as good as its execution. If your idea is going to take an extra twenty hours a week to accomplish, who is going to do it and how will you inspire them to take the lead? If you are busy working 50 hours a week then someone else needs to either lead the project or take over your tasks. Have this mapped out early so you know if you need to drop other projects, redefine tasks for your staff, or hire more people.

Using this change plan can help create the foundation for successful growth. It can also provide focus and insight on any the challenges. Change can be exciting in the beginning but that excitement often drops when people hit the first hurdle. While change is exciting, many people forget that change is not always easy. It takes persistence and determination to move forward.

Conclusion
Vansevenant Checklist

Below I have repeated the questions in a simplified list, without their descriptions. Now that you understand why each question is important you can use this list when someone brings an idea for change.

Does this change align with your business ethos?

Is the change about you?

Is it crucial to the success of the business, or would it be just "nice to have"?

Has there been demand for this change? If so, when, where, and by whom?

How does this change benefit your customers?

How will you make a profit from this?

Can the change be leveraged in multiple ways?

Can you enlist resources from outside your circle to get this done?

How much will this cost to do?

What will it cost if we do not make this change?

Are we achieving this change already?

How will you inspire and empower your staff to make this change?

Acknowledgements

I probably owe you a hug. Or a drink.

This is the hardest part to write. Everyone in my life could have played a role in writing this book. I have had people who helped writing, proof reading, editing, and or just being a sounding board for some of my ideas. I've trusted thousands of different people through Facebook, Twitter, Instagram, and Tumblr to lead me to some amazing pieces of research and content that led to many ideas in this book. There is no way I could possibly remember everyone and call them all out by name. So, if you feel that I may have forgotten you then I ask you to do me a favor. Next time you see me, tell me that I owe you a hug. Or a drink. I'll be happy to do either.

Along with the acknowledgements in the preface I'd like to mention the following people from Specialized: Frank Aldorf, Bryan Ward, Joe Wheadon, Ben Capron, Patty Young, Stweart Morton, Emma Mackie, Jesus Brenno, Andrew McGregor, Sean Xie, Pong Su, Juanse Ocampo, Johannes Sall, Mads Dellgren, Antoine Lyard, Sylvain Badia, Sebastian Maag, Viktor Armbruster, Darrick Subrata, Silvio Coatto, Koji Wantanabe, Simon Yeong, Agustin Urena, Arturo Pena, Thom Van Dulmen, Peter Kraaijvanger, Rowan Van Lier, Nick Van der Linden, Tigran Korkotyan, Pavel Stedry, Roman Fisnar, Bartosz Bilozor, Anton Kruglov, Marko Peserl, Vijay Varadarajulu, Harry Orr, Fanie Kok, Peet Le Roux, Dongkeon Lee, Dennies Bang, Carlos Arrebola, David Martin, James Chiu, Penny Chou, Jerry Chan, Richard "Neon" Salaman, David Alexander, Mark Murphy, Perry Jamieson, and Gabriel Firpo, Sam Monardo, Larry Koury, Eugene Fierkens, Eric Koh Wai Tuan, Santiago Botero, Lars Hjort, David Votava, Herve Delarbre, John Glett, Ermanno Leonardi, Hideki "Mochi" Mochizuki, Joao Firma, Abel Robles, Frank Van Dulmen, Tony

Smith, Bobby Behan, Mark Kee, Zdenek Loffelmann, Ryan French, Miguel Rojo, Olivia Chen, Richard Hemmington, Joe Brunetti, Jesse Porter, Bill Schoumann, Kim Price, Jenny Beier, Laura Wilson, Sylvia Hartmann, Julie Taillefer, Kristin Ketilsdottir, Sarge Luo, Fung Tong, Sandy Li, Carolina Rodriguez, Radka Koudelova, Kristian Pardorf, Anja Bodenmueller, Yann Noce, Thomas Lecoq, David Heine, Marco Cislaghi, Shuhei Sato, David Park, Victoria Weinberger, Victoria Oviedo, Becca Escobar, Bianca Grobbelaar, Yuriy Tomas, Cindy Liao, Emily Bennett, James Booth, Anne Immelman, Justin Sullivan, Dan Quick, Heather McFadden, Nichole Perrin, Tom Larter, Erin Sprague, Olivia Bleitz, Rita Borelli, Amy Shreve, Sam Benedict, Annette Blackham, Katie Sue Gruener, Clayton Anderson, Keriann Molloy, Aaron Vogel, Keely Shannon... and there are literally 1000 more people who could be on this list. Literally. Thank you all.

The IBRs that knowingly, or unknowingly, helped me put this book together. YoJimbo's Garage, On The Route, Recycle, Bike World, Rasmussen Bike Shop, Kyle's Bikes, Surf City Cyclery, West End Bicycles, River City Bicycles, Mike's Bikes, Wheatridge Cyclery, Faster, One on One, Ride Studio Café, Bow Cycles, Chain Reaction, Wiggle, Evans Cycles, Mellow Johnny's, Erik's Bike and Board, Village Bike & Fitness, Mack Cycles, Bow Cycle, Concept Cyclery, West End Bikes PDX, Bicycle Gallery, Bike Barn, Rock-N-Road Cyclery, Cycle Sport Concepts, Bicycle Habitat, BikeSource, Kinetic Cycles, Action Wheels, Ash Hall Cycles, Berry Mountain Cycles, Bike Gallery, Gerk's Ski and Cycle, Bike Ride, Bike Society, Cognition, Drift Bikes, Carolina Tri, Landry's Bicycles, Hampton Cycles, Jet Cycles, Sugar Cycles, Manly Cycles, Planet Cycles, Pump N Pedals, Cynergy Cycles, NorCal Bike Sport, Peloton Cycles, Two Wheel Tango, Epic Bike & Sport, Mesa Cycles, High Desert Bicycles, Two Wheeler Dealer, Bingham Cyclery, Bicycle Station, High Roller Cyclery Inc, Bike Masters, Bay Bikes, Bicycles Plus, Stevens Bicycle Shop, Cognition Cyclery, Roaring Mouse Cycles,

Perry Rubber Bike Shop, The Bike Peddler, Scotts Valley Cycle Sport, Performance Cyclery, Cycleton Denver, Brandywine Cyclery, Big Wheel Bicycles, George's Cycles and Fitness, The Bike Surgeon, Gray Goat Sports, Family Bike, Valley Bike and Ski Werks, Twenty20 Cycling Company, Main Street Bicycles, Nicollet Bike Shop, Bicycle Sports, Big Sky Bikes, Motion Makers, Marty's Reliable, Las Vegas Cyclery, Cycles Plus of Huntington, Tom's Pro Bike, Pro Bikes LLC, Dark Horse Cycles, Main Line Cycles, Firehouse Cycles, Bike Zoo, Bountiful Bicycle Center, Planet Cycles, The Cyclery, Fitzroy Revolution, Top Gear Cycles, Total Rush, Velofix, Wembley Cucles, Woolys Wheels, Cyclezone, Echelon Cyclery, Habitat Sports, iRide, Mitchell Cycles, Mt. Eden Cycles, John Beasley Cycles, CS of Covent Garden, CS Harrogate, CS Kingston, CS Birmingham, CS Ruislip, CS Nottingham, CS Stafford, CS Chelmsford, CS Chester, CS Newbury, CS Plymouth, and the thousands more. Thank you all for the work you do.

The companies that support and serve the industry, many of which I referenced in the book. National Bicycle Dealers Association, Bicycle Retailer and Industry News, Bike Biz, The Mann Group, Harry Friedman and The Friedman Group, Gluskin Townley Group, USA Cycling, UCI, Shimano, SRAM, Trek Bicycles, Giant Bicycles, and Cannondale Bicycles. Thank you all for taking the time to do the research and learn about the business of bike retailer. You are all a blessing to the game.

Thanks to the crew at Starbucks, a home away from home through the writing of this book.

References & Notes

"How did people do this before the internet?!"
- Donny Perry

I Was Just Riding Along

1. Surf City Cyclery. Surfcitycyclery.com. 7470 Edinger Avenue. Huntington Beach, California 92647

2, 3. The U.S. Speciality Bicycle Retail Channel 2013 Study and Report. Prepared by The Gluskin Townley Group LLC on behalf of NBDA, National Bicycle Dealers Association. Additional data (years 2000-2004) from NBDA Industry Overview. A Look at the Bicycle Industry's Vital Statistics http://nbda.com/articles/industry-overview-2012-pg34.htm

4. US Department of Transportation Federal Highway Administration. Summary of Highway Provisions. 2012

5. National Center for Transit Research. A Return on Investment Analysis of Bikes-on-Bus Programs. 2005

6. Gasbuddy.com - http://www.gasbuddy.com/gb_retail_price_chart.aspx

7. Specialized: http://moneyweek.com/entrepreneurs-my-first-million-mike-sinyard-specialized-45339/ and Specialized.com. Trek: http://www.fundinguniverse.com/company-histories/trek-bicycle-corporation-history/ and Trekbicycles.com. Giant: http://www.giant-bicycles.com/en-us/aboutgiant/

8. USA Triathlon demographics.
http://www.usatriathlon.org/about-multisport/demographics.aspx

9. USA Cycling and the USA Cycling Development Foundation Annual Report. 2012.
https://s3.amazonaws.com/USACWeb/forms/media/2012-USA-Cycling-Annual-Report.pdf

10. Evans Cycles, evanscycles.com. The Ride of Your Life survey.
http://blog.evanscycles.com/other_stuff/the-ride-of-your-life/

11. Wall Street Journal. After Decades of Toil, Web Sales Remain Small for Many Retailers by Shelly Banjo and Paul Ziobro. 2013.
http://online.wsj.com/news/articles/SB10001424127887324906304579039101568397122

12. Spoken statement (c. 1903); published in Harper's Monthly. September 1932

13. Thomas Alva Edison : Sixty Years of an Inventor's Life (1908) by Francis Arthur Jones, p. 14

14. Pinkbike's Burning Question – Should You Support Your Local Bike Shop or Buy Online? By Mike Kazmer. January 2013.
http://www.pinkbike.com/news/Pinkbikes-Burning-Question-shop-local-or-online-2013.html

15. Bicycle Retailer and Industry News. Fred Clements: A Formula for High-Profit Bike Stores. A blog by NBDA Executive Director Fred Clements. June, 2013.
http://www.bicycleretailer.com/opinion-analysis/2013/06/14/blog-formula-high-profit-bike-stores#.UtGJq_RDuSo

16. ride-faster.com

17. ridestudiocafe.com

18. Gallup Politics. Congress Retains Low Honest Rating. Nurses have high honesty rating; car salespeople, lowest. By Frank Newport. December 2012. http://www.gallup.com/poll/159035/congress-retains-low-honesty-rating.aspx

19. Tedx Pugent Sound. Simon Sinek, How Great Leaders Inspire Action. May 2010. http://www.ted.com/talks/simon_sinek_how_great_leaders_inspire_action.html. Ted Blog: The 20 Most Popular Ted Talks As Of This Moment by Kate Torgovnick May. December 2013. http://blog.ted.com/2013/12/16/the-most-popular-20-ted-talks-2013/

20. Investopedia.com, Sales Per Square Foot. http://www.investopedia.com/terms/s/sales-per-square-foot.asp

21. The U.S. Speciality Bicycle Retail Channel 2013 Study and Report. Prepared by The Gluskin Townley Group LLC on behalf of NBDA, National Bicycle Dealers Association.

22. USA Today. The 9 Most Successful Retail Stores in the USA by Trey Thoelcke and Michael B. Sauter, 24/7 Wall St. November 2012. http://www.usatoday.com/story/money/business/2012/11/18/most-successful-retail-stores/1710571/

23. The U.S. Speciality Bicycle Retail Channel 2013 Study and Report. Prepared by The Gluskin Townley Group LLC on behalf of NBDA, National Bicycle Dealers Association.

24. Wim Vansevenant. http://en.wikipedia.org/wiki/Wim_Vansevenant

I visited Surf City in January or February of 2012, great group of guys.

The bike shops I was working at when I had my most memorable JRA moments were On The Route in Chicago, IL (1) and Bike World in Des Moines, IA (2 & 3).

According to Gasbuddy.com the national average for US gas prices in January of 2004 was approximately $1.50/gallon. By January 2014 it rose to $3.33/gallon. The highest national average gas prices in the past decade were recorded in the summer of 2008 at $4.12/gallon.

To get a "Support Your Local Bike Shop" t-shirt check out 1664 BMX Distribution out of Edmonton, Alberta.

Just a few online retailers that offer everything to become a cyclist: performancebike.com, competitivecyclist.com, wiggle.com, and chainreaction.com.

I have visited over 500 bike retailers in over 20 countries. Those countries are: Canada, USA, Mexico, Brazil, Uruguay, Portugal, Spain, France, Germany, Italy, Netherlands, United Kingdom, Czech, South Africa, China, South Korea, Japan, Singapore, Australia, and New Zealand.

The best way I have seen to store brake/shift cables is in a 6' tall PVC tube. Standing upright with a hole cut in the center of the tube. The cables stand upright and consume less than one square foot of floor space. I saw this at River City Bicycles in Portland, OR.

According to Wikipedia, Kansas City Shuffle is a tune by jazz pianist Bennie Moten. It was recorded by his jazz band "Bennie Moten's Kansas City Orchestra" on 13 December 1926 in Chicago, Illinois and originally released by Victor Records. However, I am taking the reference from the 2006 movie Lucky Number Slevin starring Josh Hartnett, Bruce Willis, Lucy Liu, Morgan Freeman, and Ben Kingsley. Urban Dictionary has the best definition of the Kansas City Shuffle, "You look left and Bruce Willis snaps your neck."

I have visited Wheatridge Cyclery in Denver Colorado twice, both times in 2012. I have yet to go to Faster in Scottsdale, Arizona and took their store information from their website. I visited One on

One in May of 2007. I haven't visited Ride Studio Café in Lexington but am really looking forward to.

According to Wikipedia a "catch-22" is a paradoxical situation from which an individual cannot escape because of contradictory rules.

The Timmy moniker was first invented at the 2012 Specialized Dealer Event during a presentation I gave titled Uncommon Service. It was not a reference to Timmy Burch, the character from South Park.

At the time of writing these notes, Simon Sinek's Ted Talk had received 14,228,854 views.

The title and the idea of "Retail Industry or Real Estate Industry" came from an interview Mitch Joel conducted with Doug Stephens on the podcast, Six Pixels of Separation. It was episode #364, titled Peeking Into the Future of Retail with Doug Stephens and it came out on June 30th, 2013.

The Wim Vansevenant story is amazing.

Time for Phase 2:
Pricing & Pareto

1. CNN Money. 10 Big Dot.com Flops by David Goldman. 2010. http://money.cnn.com/galleries/2010/technology/1003/gallery.d ot_com_busts/9.html

2. Comedy Central. South Park, Gnomes. Season 2, episode 17. 1998 http://southpark.wikia.com/wiki/Underpants_Gnomes

3. PBS.org, Who Made America? John Wanamaker. http://www.pbs.org/wgbh/theymadeamerica/whomade/wanama ker_hi.html and http://en.wikipedia.org/wiki/John_Wanamaker

4. Retail Info Systems News. Smart Quotes: Inside the Best Minds in Retail. By Joe Skorupa. October 2013. http://m.risnews.edgl.com/BlogDetailPage?BlogId=684&Flag=1. Peter Fader, Frances and Pei-Yuan Chia Profession of Marketing, The Wharton School of the University of Pennsylvania. http://www.upenn.edu/almanac/v50/n32/pf.html

5. Charles Duhigg. http://charlesduhigg.com/the-power-of-habit/

6. Harvard Business Review. How to Stop Customers from Fixating on Price by Marco Bertini and Luc Wathieu. May 2010. http://hbr.org/2010/05/how-to-stop-customers-from-fixating-on-price/ar/1 . Michelin Tires: www.michelinman.com

7. Vilfredo Pareto: http://en.wikipedia.org/wiki/Vilfredo_Pareto and the Pareto Principle (80/20 Rule): http://en.wikipedia.org/wiki/Pareto_principle

Kozmo.com was a VC-driven online company that promised free one-hour delivery of videos, games, DVDs, music, magazines, books, food, basics & and Starbucks coffee. The slogan for Kozmo.com was "We'll be right over."

South Park is produced by Comedy Central. I absolutely love the view that South Park takes on pop culture. I presented the Underpants Gnomes business model and how it relates to bike retailers at the 2013 Specialized Dealer Event. It was the first time anyone had ever played clips from South Park during one of these events.

The "Pricing Is…" list was borrowed from a loose outline presented by Mark Stiving PhD at the 2013 Interbike in Las Vegas, NV. The presentation was titled Impact Pricing: Your Blueprint for Driving Profits. My list is only a portion of the list that Stiving referenced.

Owners and managers that provide discounts while prohibiting their employees to do so is one of the most common reasons these owners and managers feel they could never leave the business. Of course this is true! Customers will wait in line for the person who can provide the best price, meaning te owner and manager can never leave.

When to put items on sale is every retailer's decision. I have seen retailers that will put it on sale if it doesn't move within the first 90 days, I have also seen retailers hold on to a product for nearly a decade. Waiting for the one person in the world looking for a 9-speed, size 63, road bike in celeste green. My recommendations are only recommendations, not a must-do. I encourage each retailer to find what works best for them.

While manufacturers will make the product it is ultimately the retailer's responsibility to sell it. Retailers should not expect the manufacturers to provide detailed analysis of their product, competitive reports, or how-to-sell tips.

Vilfredo Pareto never used the term "80/20". That term was coined by management guru and author Joseph M. Juran in 1937. Juran died in 2008, he was 103.

Not everything is 80/20 and no retailer should blindly follow the 80/20 rule in everything. Ignoring the tip of the iceberg is ignoring 20% of the business and potential areas where things may go wrong.

Tutorial on how to perform a Pareto Analysis in Excel: http://www.excel-easy.com/examples/pareto-chart.html

Checklists, Scheduling, Hours, & Brown M&Ms

1. Crazy From The Heat by David Lee Roth. Published by Hyperion. Reprint in December 1998.

2. David Lee Roth explains the Brown M&Ms. http://bit.ly/1cV2bJS

3. The Checklist Manifesto: How to Get Things Right by Atul

Gawande. Published by Picador 2009

4. World Health Organization (WHO) surgical safety checklist and implementation manual. By the World Alliance for Patient Safety. 2008.
http://www.who.int/patientsafety/safesurgery/ss_checklist/en/

5. Soda Head. What time do you typically leave work each night. (survey) April 2012. http://www.sodahead.com/living/what-time-do-you-typically-leave-work-each-night/question-2599811/

6. Fifty percent of the stores studied were Specialized Concept Stores. The remaining 50% were not Specialized retailers nor were they concept stores of any other brand.

7. According to the Bike Fix website they are also open Monday-Wednesday and Friday from 9am to 2pm. Saturdays are the day they staff up heavily for their customers.
http://www.bikefix.co.nz/

I presented the story of Van Halen and the brown M&Ms at the 2012 Specialized Dealer Event in Colorado and the 2012 Australian and New Zealand Dealer Event in Cairns. I gave everyone in the audiences a handful of brown M&Ms. Of course with brown ones removed.

David Lee Roth's contract had a lot more cool stuff than no brown M&Ms. He also asked for cigarettes, 12 assorted Danon yogurts on ice, three bottles of Jack Daniels, one bottle of Southern Comfort, two bottles of Blue Nun white wine, herring in sour cream, and one large tube of KY Jelly. Roth also embellished the size of his contract, it was not as big as a "Chinese phone book" as he claims. It was only 42 pages long with single spacing.

One of my favorite questions on the WHO checklist is, "Is the site marked?" I imagine a time when someone went in for a knee surgery and everything was performed perfectly, if they hadn't performed surgery on the wrong knee. That is when the question made it to the checklist.

The highest and lowest labor rates I have ever seen for bike retail (meaning I have seen the books and not just had someone tell me what theirs was). 29% which was found at a retailer in Brazil and 9% from a retailer in the US. In both cases I would not recommend it as a goal. The Brazilian retailer was too overstaffed- a cultural and political issue for businesses all over Brazil. The US retailer was understaffed to the point of sacrificing quality customer service.

The Timmy Factor

1. How to Get People to Do Stuff by Susan Weinschenk PhD. Published by New Riders. http://theteamw.com/

2. Wall Street Journal. To Motivate Staffers, Are Carrots Better Than Sticks? By Alan Murray. March 2010. http://online.wsj.com/news/articles/SB10001424052748703315004575073270727383294

3. Harvard Business Review. The High Cost of Low Wages by Wayne F. Cascio. December 2006. http://hbr.org/2006/12/the-high-cost-of-low-wages/ar/1

4. United States Department of Labor. Bureau of Labor Statistics. Occupational Outlook Handbook, retail sales workers summary. 2012 http://www.bls.gov/oes/current/oes412031.htm

5. TEDxCambridge. The Good Jobs Strategy presented by Zeynep Ton. 2013 http://tedxtalks.ted.com/video/The-Good-Jobs-Strategy-Zeynep-T;search%3Atag%3A%22TEDxCambridge%22

6. The Good Jobs Strategy: How the Smartest Companies Invest in Employees to Lower Costs and Boost Profits by Zeynep Ton. Published by New Harvest.

7. Specialized offers training through Specialized Bicycle Components University or SBCU. Park Tool offers training through the Park Tool Tech Summit http://www.parktool.com/techsummit. SRAM offers training through SRAM Technical University or STU.

8. Switch: How to Change Things When Change is Hard by Chip Heath & Dan Heath. http://heathbrothers.com/books/switch/

9. Business Insider. 18 Facts About McDonald's that Will Blow Your Mind by Gus Lubin and Mamta Badkar. April 2012. http://www.businessinsider.com/19-facts-about-mcdonalds-that-will-blow-your-mind-2012-4?op=1

10. About McDonalds. Day in the Life of a Restaurant Employee: How McDonald's was built on a culture of operations and focuses on Fast, Accurate, Friendly, and Fries. July 2012. http://community.aboutmcdonalds.com/t5/Let-s-Talk/A-Day-in-the-Life-of-a-Restaurant-Employee-How-McDonald-s-was/ba-p/852

There are always tires that need to be inflated. I get frustrated when I see people standing around in a bike shop. Inflating tires, wiping down bikes, stocking product, cleaning, etc. Always something to be done and always something to prepare for.
There are two cycles of labor, a vicious cycle and a virtuous cycle. If you pay poorly what kind of work quality can you expect? Poor. If the work quality is poor what level of customer service are you capable offering? Poor. If customer service is poor how profitable will be? Not very. If you're not profitable how much can you pay the staff? Nothing. This is a vicious cycle. To make it a virtuous cycle simply start by asking if you pay great what kind of work quality can you expect?

In writing this I learned that some people believe that the saying "if you pay peanuts you get monkeys" is racist. I do not believe this is true. What I do believe is that no one can please the PC police.

Managing Technicians

1. Monty Python's Flying Circus. How to Recognise Different Types of Trees From Quite a Long Way Away. October 1969

2. Bicycle Retailer and Industry News. Fred Clements: A Formula for High-Profit Bike Stores. A blog by NBDA Executive Director Fred Clements. June, 2013.
http://www.bicycleretailer.com/opinion-analysis/2013/06/14/blog-formula-high-profit-bike-stores#.UtGJq_RDuSo

3. Show Love, showloveworld.com, https://vimeo.com/36258512. 718 Cyclery: http://www.718c.com/

4. Salary.com, http://swz.salary.com/SalaryWizard/Bicycle-Repairer-Job-Description.aspx

5. The U.S. Speciality Bicycle Retail Channel 2013 Study and Report. Prepared by The Gluskin Townley Group LLC on behalf of NBDA, National Bicycle Dealers Association.

6. Tom Sachs: http://tenbullets.com/ and http://www.tomsachs.org/

7. Wikipedia: Knolling: http://en.wikipedia.org/wiki/Knoll_(verb)

8. Grinding It Out: The Making of McDonald's by Ray Croc. Publsihed by Henry Regnery Company. May 1977

9. Bike Biz. Growth Job of the Future: Bike Mechanic by Carlton Reid. October 2012. http://www.bikebiz.com/news/read/growth-job-of-the-future-bike-mechanic/013781

10. Bloomberg Businessweek Politics and Policy. What Tomorrow's Jobs Look Like by Elizabeth Dwoskin. Novembr 2012.

11. New York Times. Using Menu Psychology to Entice Diners by Sarah Kershaw. December 2009. http://www.nytimes.com/2009/12/23/dining/23menus.html?pag ewanted=all&_r=0

12. Cornell University School of Hotel Administration. $ or Dollars: Efftcs of Menu-price Formats on Restaurant Checks. By Sybil S. Yang, Sheryl E. Kimes PhD, and Mauro M Sessarego. http://www.hotelschool.cornell.edu/research/chr/pubs/reports/a bstract-15048.html

13. Ditch Dare Do: 3D Personal branding for Executives by William Arruda. Published Trade Mark Press. April 2013.

Monty Python's Bicycle Repairman sketch: http://www.youtube.com/watch?v=rxfzm9dfqBw

The results from Salary.com do take into account people who submit their salaries. However, I have also found that the title someone carries correlates to their potential salary. Meaning, if a person wasn't called a Bicycle Technician but instead carried the title of Director of Service, salary estimates go up not just online, but also when moving on to the next job. Crazy to think that earning more money could be done with a title change.

Tom Sachs' video Ten Bullets is brilliant. I also recommend his video on sweeping. I have never been so enthralled by the process of sweeping. Awesome stuff.

For some inspiration or examples of knolling start by searching #alwaysbeknolling on Instagram.

You can find Erik's at eriksbikeshop.com and Mike's Bikes at mikesbikes.com

I believe travel coordination and bike trips are an underserved opportunity for bike retailers. If the IBR was able to sell the bike, fit the bike, service the bike, provide coaching, and then provide the experience of riding somewhere amazing then they control the entire cycling experience. With that, nearly every cycling thought would default to that store.

Bloomberg Businessweek made the prediction that bicycle technician is a growing industry based on the amount the US DOT is allocating toward bike lanes (790 million). It also says that the average salary for a bike technician is $23,660. Roughly $2000 more than the Salary.com calculations.

The phrase "What would you say you do here?" is quoting Bob from the movie Office Space. In a movie of amazing one-liners, this is the one I have repeated the most.

Managing Leadouts

1. Fleishman Hillard. 2012 Digital Influence Index Shows Internet as Leading Influence in Consumer Purchasing Choices. January 2012. http://fleishmanhillard.com/2012/01/news-and-opinions/2012-digital-influence-index-shows-internet-as-leading-influence-in-consumer-purchasing-choices/

2. Glengarry Glen Ross. October 1992. http://www.imdb.com/title/tt0104348/

3. NPR. Death of the (Predatory) Salesman: These Days, It's A Buyer's Market. Author interview with Daniel Pink. December 2012. http://www.npr.org/2012/12/31/168132488/death-of-the-predatory-salesman-these-days-its-a-buyers-market

4. DO. The pursuit of xceptional execution by Kevin Kelly. http://photo.goodreads.com/documents/1381865743books/18587427.pdf

5, 6. ComScore / E-Tailing Group surveys, cited in Konana research about external reviews effect on purchasing decisions

7. The Mobile Movement. Understanding Smartphone Users. By thinkmobile with Google. April 2011. http://www.gstatic.com/ads/research/en/2011_TheMobileMovement.pdf

8. Business Insider. Pinterest Is Powering A Huge Amount Of Social Commerce, And Twitter Isn't Too Shabby Either. By Cooper Smith. October 2013. http://www.businessinsider.com/twitter-and-pinterest-in-social-commerce-2013-10

9. Principles of Bicycle Retailing III: All New Strategies for the 90s and Beyond. By Randy W. Kirk. Published by Info Net Pub

In 1998 I was living in Chicago and there was an 18-month period where there were three Starbucks at the intersection of Clyborn and Webster. One on the NW corner, which according to Google, is still there. One on the SE corner that is gone. And one that was in the Barnes & Noble on the SW corner- which, since it is inside B&N, if it is still there then I can imagine it won't be there too much longer.

For a long time I was an advocate of solution sales methods. To the point that I worked closely with Harry Friedman and The Friedman Group. If you want to see me and Harry talk about sales processes check some of this action out: http://www.youtube.com/user/donnyalexanderperry

Rico Suave was a huge influence on my childhood. While his music only lasted a summer, I wore bandanas for almost a year.

I indirectly got the idea for using specific words from Apple. Their Genius Bar training teaches people the words and their connotation. However, it is incredibly difficult to get a copy of an Apple training manual. If anyone reading this has one, I'd love to read it.

Marketing the IBR

1. Statistic Brain. January 2014.
http://www.statisticbrain.com/facebook-statistics/

2. Statistic Brain. January 2014.
http://www.statisticbrain.com/twitter-statistics/

3. Statistic Brain. November 2013.
http://www.statisticbrain.com/instagram-company-statistics/

4. Strava does not share total users. This data is based on the assumption that a user's profile number is the number of active users the platform had when they signed up. If the user profile is http://www.strava.com/athletes/169922 then they were the 169,922nd person to create an account on the platform.

5. Jab, Jab, Jab, Right Hook: How to Tell Your Story in a Noisy Social World by Gary Vaynerchuk. Published by Harper Business, November 2013

6. Search Metrics. SEO Ranking Factors – Rank Correlation 2013 for Google USA.
http://www.searchmetrics.com/en/services/ranking-factors-2013/

7. Statistic Brain. January 2014.
http://www.statisticbrain.com/facebook-statistics/

8. CNet. Hitwise: 1 in 5 U.S. pageviews belong to Facebook. By Josh Lowensohn. February 2012. http://news.cnet.com/8301-1023_3-57370786-93/hitwise-1-in-5-u.s-pageviews-belong-to-facebook/

9. The Social Habit. Is Facebook Replacing the Morning Cup Of Coffee? By Mark Schaeffer. September 2012.
http://socialhabit.com/uncategorized/our-morning-habit/

10. Inside Facebook. Studies Show More Than 40 Percent Decreased Organic Reach on Facebook. By Justin Lafferty. December 2013. http://www.insidefacebook.com/2013/12/23/studies-show-more-than-40-percent-decreased-organic-reach-on-facebook/

11. Buffer Blog. A Scientific Guide to Posting Tweets, Facebook Posts, Emails and Blog posts at thebest time. By Belle Beth Cooper. August 2013. http://blog.bufferapp.com/best-time-to-tweet-post-to-facebook-send-emails-publish-blogposts

12. The Social Habit. Is Facebook Replacing the Morning Cup Of Coffee? By Mark Schaeffer. September 2012. http://socialhabit.com/uncategorized/our-morning-habit/

13. Statistic Brain. January 2014. http://www.statisticbrain.com/twitter-statistics/

14. Gigaom. NPR host's live-tweeting of his mother's last moment shows the power of 140 characters. By Mathew Ingram. July 2013. http://gigaom.com/2013/07/29/npr-hosts-live-tweeting-of-his-mothers-last-moments-shows-the-power-of-140-characters/

15. The Social Habit. Are Consumer Expectations for Social Customer Service Realistic? By Jay Baer. October 2012. http://socialhabit.com/uncategorized/customer-service-expectations/

16. BBC News Norfolk. #Bloodycyclists Twitter Post Driver Emma Way Guilty. November 2013.

17. Statistic Brain. November 2013. http://www.statisticbrain.com/instagram-company-statistics/

18. Casey Neistat. Instagram I Love You. October, 2012. http://www.youtube.com/watch?v=GacoqdKjVyE

19. Buffer Blog. 8 Surprising New Instagram Statistics to Get the Most out of the Picture Social Netowrk. By Sabel Harris. October 2013. http://blog.bufferapp.com/instagram-stats-instagram-tips

20. Social Media Examiner. 26 Tips for Using Instagram for Business. By Debbie Hemley. September 2013. http://www.socialmediaexaminer.com/instagram-for-business-tips/

21. Buffer Blog. 8 Surprising New Instagram Statistics to Get the Most out of the Picture Social Netowrk. By Sabel Harris. October 2013. http://blog.bufferapp.com/instagram-stats-instagram-tips

22. Strava. http://www.strava.com

23. Bicycling South Africa. Girl-On-A-Bike's Blog: Addicted to Strava! By Lesley-Anne Mallon. September 2013. http://www.bicycling.co.za/blogs/girl-bikes-blog-addicted-strava/

Marketing means only doing two things. A positive connection with customers and being extremely helpful. I learned the first from Mitch Joel and the second from Gary Vaynerchuk. Check them out.

I had been trying to get a solid number on how many users Strava had and the people at Strava would not budge. There is nothing online. Then I remembered that when you create a segment, create a route, or upload a ride each one is given a number, example: strava.com/segments/639812. When Strava launched ROUTES I was one of the first people to use it. The first route I created was my commute (#88) and the second route I created a few minutes later was the Specialized Lunch Ride (#90). Made me think, could Strava be posting their total number of users as the profile URL? And it sure looks like it. I read that the first six accounts created were dummy accounts. Co-founders Kitchel and Gainey are #7 and #10, former CEO Horvath is #57, and I am #169,922.

Facebook, Twitter, Instagram, Strava... these are digital companies going through some extremely fast growth curves. They change things all the time. There is a good chance that one year after this is published the stats or functions I discuss of these platforms will have changed. Writing about social platforms doesn't have the greatest shelf life.

If you're looking for some quick tips on Facebook check out this slideshow I put together: http://www.slideshare.net/donnyperry/be-awesome-at-facebook

The RPM method for content creation was a spinoff of RPJ from Dan and Ian at TropicalMBA.com. They chose Rip, Pivot, and Jam. I thought Rip, Pivot, and Move made the acronym more cycling friendly. You might say that I RPM'd their RPJ system.

Might notice that my calendar is heavier with road events than mountain. My bad, I'm a roadie- all highway.

Looking Forward

1. University Transport Research Center. Analysis of Bicycling Trends and policies in Large North American Cities: Lessons for New York. Prepared by John Pucher and Ralph Buehler. March 2011. http://grist.files.wordpress.com/2011/04/analysis-bike-final1.pdf

2. US Census Bureau 2011. 158.3m females to 153.3 males in the US. http://www.infoplease.com/spot/womencensus1.html

3. Huffington Post. Minorities in America: Whites Losing Majority in Under-5 Age Group. By Hope Yen. June 2013. http://www.huffingtonpost.com/2013/06/13/minorities-in-america-census_n_3432369.html

4. Forbes. Why Millennials Are Spnding More Than They Earn, And Parents Are Footing The Bill. By Larissa Faw. May 2012.

http://www.forbes.com/sites/larissafaw/2012/05/18/why-millennials-are-spending-more-than-they-earn/

5. US Census Bureau 2012. State & Country Quick Facts. http://quickfacts.census.gov/qfd/states/00000.html

6. Los Angeles Times. What's in Millennial's Wallets? By Emily Alpert. May 2013. http://articles.latimes.com/2013/may/18/local/la-me-credit-cards-millennials-20130519

7. NPR. Educated And Jobless: What's Next For Millennials? By NPR Staff. November 2011. http://www.npr.org/2011/11/12/142274437/educated-and-jobless-whats-next-for-millenials

8. Bike Biz. Gluskin Towley Group: Bike Boom Coming in 2020. By Mark Sutton. November 2013. http://www.bikebiz.com/news/read/gluskin-townley-group-bike-boom-coming-in-2020/015732

9. U.S. PIRG. Young People Driving Less, Embrace Other Transportation. By Larry Copeland. October 2013. http://www.uspirg.org/media/usp/young-people-driving-less-embrace-other-transportation

10. US Department of Labor, US Bureau of Statistics. Women in the Labor Force: A Databook. December 2011. http://www.bls.gov/cps/wlf-databook-2011.pdf

11. Huffington Post. The 11 Cities Where Women Out-Earn Men. By Nathaniel Cahners Hindman. September 2010, Updated May 2011. http://www.huffingtonpost.com/2010/09/02/women-outearn-men_n_703503.html#s133830title=Atlanta_Georgia

12. Institute of Educational Sciences. National Center for Education Statistics. Degrees conferred by degree-granting

institutions, by level of degree and sex of student:
http://nces.ed.gov/programs/digest/d07/tables/dt07_258.asp

13. Marketing Charts. Women in mature Economies Control
Household Spending. May 2010.
http://www.marketingcharts.com/topics/asia-pacific/women-in-
mature-economies-control-household-spending-12931/

14. The League of American Bicyclists. Women On A Roll.
Benchmarking Women's Bicycling in the United States – and five
keys to get more women on wheels. Carolyn Szczepanski. August,
2013.
http://www.bikeleague.org/sites/lab.huang.radicaldesigns.org/file
s/WomenBikeReport(web).pdf

15. Gluskin Townley Group. Fewer males and more females are
participating in bicycling! September 2013. Collected and posted
by The League of American Bicyclists, News from The League.
September 2013. By Carolyn Szczepanski.
http://bikeleague.org/content/fewer-men-more-women-riding

16. About.com. how to Work With A Bike Shop. Find a Good Store
Then Help Them Help You. By David Fiedler.
http://bicycling.about.com/od/bikemaintenance/tp/How-To-
Work-With-A-Bike-Shop.htm

17. Mastering the Uphill Shift. The Intimidation Factor. By Anna
Doorenbos.
https://masteringtheuphillshift.wordpress.com/tag/female-
cyclist/

18. Tribes: We Need You to Lead Us. By Seth Godin. Published
October 2008. http://sethgodin.com/sg/books.asp

19. Brand Hijack: Marketing Without Marketing. By Alex
Wipperfurth. Published by Portfolio Trade, October 2006.

20. The New York Times. The Marketing of No Marketing. By Rob Walker. June, 2003.
http://www.nytimes.com/2003/06/22/magazine/the-marketing-of-no-marketing.html?pagewanted=all&src=pm

21. Messenger Institute for Media Accuracy. Team PUMA Hits the Streets. PUMA Cycling Team formed from New York City Bike Messengers. July, 2004. http://www.messarchives.com/040723-puma.html

22. Bern. http://www.bernunlimited.com/portfolio/kevin-bolger-squid/

23. Premium Rush. Columbia Pictures. Released August 2012.
http://www.imdb.com/title/tt1547234

24. New York Post. Shooting the Messengers by Chris Erikson. August, 2012. http://nypost.com/2012/08/19/shooting-the-messengers/

25. The New York Times. The Finish Line Starts Here. By Lindsay Crouse. September, 2013.
http://www.nytimes.com/2013/09/06/nyregion/the-finish-line-starts-here.html?_r=0

26. National Sporting Goods Association. Sports Participation in the United States. 2012 Edition.
http://www.nsga.org/i4a/pages/index.cfm?pageid=4653

27. Leisure Trends, An NPD Group Company. Running Retail Market Overview.
http://www.leisuretrends.com/showarticle.aspx?id=1019 - National Bicycle Dealer Association. A Look at the Bicycle Industry's Vital Statistics. 2012. http://nbda.com/articles/industry-overview-2012-pg34.htm

28. The New York Times. Competition Gaining on Running Gear Stores. By Jan Ellen Spiegel. February, 2008.

http://www.nytimes.com/2008/02/07/business/smallbusiness/07sbiz.html?pagewanted=all

29. USA Cycling. USA Cycling Fact Sheet.
https://s3.amazonaws.com/USACWeb/forms/media/2012-Fact-Sheet.pdf   USA Cycling Active Member Demographics:
http://www.usacycling.org/corp/demographics.php

30. 2013 Boston Marathon Statistics.
http://raceday.baa.org/statistics.html

31. Switch. How to Change Things when Change is Hard. By Chip Heath and Dan Heath. Published by Crown Business. February 2010. http://heathbrothers.com/books/switch/

There were 158.3 million females in the United States in 2011. The number of males was 153.3 million. At 65 and older, there were 13.3 percent more women than men in 2011.

The latest census numbers show: The population younger than 5 stood at 49.9 percent minority in 2012. The nonwhite population increased by 1.9 percent to 116 million, or 37 percent. Hispanics make up 17 percent of the U.S.; blacks, 12.3 percent; Asians, 5 percent; and multiracial Americans, 2.4 percent. About 353 of the nation's 3,143 counties, or 11 percent, are now "majority-minority," including six which tipped last year. Among the under-5 age group, 22 percent live in poverty, typically in more rural states such as Mississippi, Arkansas and Louisiana. Black toddlers were most likely to be poor, at 41 percent, followed by Hispanics at 32 percent and whites at 13 percent. Asian toddlers had a poverty rate of 11 percent.

Amazon.com was founded in 1994 in Bellevue, WA. In February of 2013 it was voted as the most trusted company in US Harris Poll.

I opted to write a section on growing the market of minorities. I tried, but struggled to find adequate research and everything I wrote just sounded racist. I believe the strategy is simple though, retailers should not live inside their walls but move beyond their brick and mortar and set up demos, pop-up stores, events, and sponsorships in neighborhoods and communities they don't normally reach. If any group of people has never come in the store, then it is time to start going to them.

I imagine that everyone working at Lululemon struggle to sell to men in the same way many bike retailers struggle to sell to women. I envision them running through courses on "how to sell to men" and "how to not intimidate men". Walking into a Lululemon, there is a corner in the back dedicated to men. I believe this "corner" helps establish Lululemon as a brand for women. Until they split their stores evenly between men and women they may never overcome that stigma. The same is true for bike retailers, dedicating a corner to women's products is adding the belief that cycling is predominantly a men's sport.

I have had hundreds of men tell me that they needed to discuss a bike purchase with their spouse. My favorite is when a customer kept referring to his wife as his CFO, or Chief Financial Officer.

I met Kevin "Squid" Bolger once. He and I were competing in an alleycat in Chicago, not sure what year though.

I hate PBR.

Leading Out Retail

A Creative Look at Bicycle Retail
and What All Retailers Can Learn From It

by Donny Perry

You can connect with the author on Twitter, @donnyperry

Thanks for reading.